Letts Numeracy Year 3

Teacher's Book

Peter Patilla &
Paul Broadbent

First published 1999

Letts Educational, Schools and Colleges Division, 9–15 Aldine Street,
London W12 8AW
Tel: (020) 8740 2270
Fax: (020) 8740 2280

British Library Cataloguing-in-Publication Data
A CIP record for this book is available from the British Library.

ISBN 1 84085 319 0
Printed and bound in Italy
Letts Educational is the trading name of BPP [Letts Educational] Ltd

Contents

UNIT	Topic	Page
	Introduction	4
	Teaching plans for Terms 1–3	5
	Term 1	
1	Place value	10
2	Addition and subtraction	11
3	Money and problems	12
4	Measures	13
5	Length	14
6	Shape and space	15
7	Review	16
8	Counting	17
9	Multiplication tables	18
10	Multiplication problems	19
11	Fractions	20
12	Subtraction and time	21
13	Graphs	22
14	Review	23
	Term 2	
1	Place value	26
2	Addition	27
3	Addition and subtraction	28
4	Money and problems	29
5	Shape and space	30
6	Time and weight	31
7	Review	32
8	Numbers and counting patterns	33
9	Addition and problems	34
10	Division	35
11	Fractions	36
12	Bar charts	37
13	Review	38
	Term 3	
1	Place value	40
2	Adding and subtracting	41
3	Problems	42
4	Adding	43
5	Capacity	44
6	Shape and space	45
7	Review	46
8	Numbers	47
9	Remainders	48
10	Money and problems	49
11	Fractions	50
12	Time and subtracting	51
13	Diagrams	52
14	Review	53
	Answers	54

Introduction

The pupil material for Year 3 consists of:

- 5 posters for Term 1
- 2 posters for Term 2
- 3 posters for Term 3
- 96-page Pupil's Book for Terms 1 to 3.

This Teacher's Book supports all pupil activities for Terms 1 to 3 and provides answers to the pupil activities.

The content of the material mirrors the suggested Medium Term Planning outlined in the support material for the National Numeracy Strategy. The content of the books follows the suggested objectives given for each unit of work very closely. The structure is based on a three-part lesson:

- mental activities and introduction to the teaching focus for the whole class
- pupil activities based on the teaching focus, either as a class or as a large group
- plenary session for the whole class.

MENTAL ACTIVITIES

The suggested mental activities are intended to be daily 10-minute sessions with the whole class. Pupils will need simple materials such as number cards for some of these activities.

TEACHING FOCUS

Tell the class what the teaching focus is to be and explain what they will be learning during the week. Use the left-hand pupil page and appropriate posters for the whole-class introduction to the topic.

Pupils should undertake tasks from the supporting activities sections of this Teacher's Book and complete the right-hand pupil pages from their books. Each page has a challenge which is more open and can provide starting points for investigation and extended activities.

References are made to the complementary series of books called *KS2 Numeracy Activity Book*.

PLENARY SESSION

At the end of each teaching block use the plenary session to recap and review, check which objectives have been understood, and use vocabulary from the Teacher's Book. The posters and left-hand pupil pages can be used for plenary sessions as well as introductions.

PUPIL PAGES

To complete some pages pupils will need access to markers such as counters. These markers will be placed on the pupil pages to indicate each pupil's responses to teacher questioning. These activities are called 'Cover Up' activities.

Cover Up activities

Cover Up activities are a powerful teaching strategy for the following reasons:

- they allow ample time for pupils to think through their response
- errors can be corrected quickly
- glancing round responses gives immediate feedback for the teacher
- watching how the markers are placed gives an indication of which strategy a pupil might be using
- teacher and pupil can choose whether a written record is required to make the cover-up response more permanent.

Teaching plan for Term 1

EVERY DAY: Practise and develop oral and mental skills (e.g. counting, mental strategies, rapid recall of +, –, × and ÷ facts)	
Read and write whole numbers up to 1000. Add/subtract 1, 10, 100 to any whole number. Count on/back in 10s, 100s from any two- and three-digit number. Recall addition and subtraction facts for each number up to at least 10. Recall pairs that make 20.	Derive doubles of whole numbers to 15, corresponding halves. Know multiplication facts in ×5 table and derive division facts. Recall multiplication facts up to 5 × 5. Recall multiplication facts in ×10 table and derive division facts. Recall multiplication facts in ×2 table and derive division facts.

Unit	Teacher's page	Pupil page	Topic	Objectives children will be taught
1	10	6–7	Place value, ordering, estimating, rounding Reading numbers from scales	Read and write whole numbers to 1000 in figures and words. Know what each digit represents and partition three-digit numbers into a multiple of 100, a multiple of 10, and ones. Read and begin to write the vocabulary of estimation. Estimate up to 100 objects. Read scales to the nearest division.
	11	8–9	Understanding + and – Mental calculation strategies (+ and –)	Extend understanding of the operations of addition and subtraction. Read and begin to write related vocabulary. Use +, – and = signs. Recognise that addition can be done in any order. Put larger number first in order to count on. Identify near doubles. Bridge through a multiple of 10 and adjust.
3	12	10–11	Money and 'real life' problems Making decisions, checking results	Recognise all coins and notes. Understand £/p. notation (e.g. £3.06). Find totals, give change and work out how to pay. Choose appropriate number operations and calculation methods to solve word problems. Explain and record methods informally. Check sums by adding in different order.
4	13	12–13	Measures, including problems	Read time to 5 minutes. Use decimal notation for *m* and *cm*. Suggest suitable units and equipment to estimate or measure lengths, including *km*. Read scales. Read and begin to write the vocabulary related to length.
5	14	14–15	Measures, including problems	Use ruler to draw and measure lines to nearest half cm. Choose an appropriate number operation and calculation method to solve word problems. Explain and record method informally. Measure and compare using *m*, *cm*. Know relationship *m*, *cm*; *km*, *m*. Record to nearest whole/half unit, or as mixed units (e.g. 3 m 20 cm).
6	15	16–17	Shape and space Reasoning about shapes	Classify and describe 3-D and 2-D shapes, referring to reflective symmetry, faces, sides/edges, vertices, angles. Read and begin to write the vocabulary of position. Use spaces on square grids. Identify right angles in 2-D shapes and in the environment. Investigate general statements about shapes.
7	16	18–19	Assess and review	

Read and write whole numbers up to 1000. Say the number that is 10, 100 more/less than any two- or three-digit number. Count on/back in 10s, 100s from any two-/three-digit number. State subtraction fact corresponding to addition fact, and vice versa. Recall addition and subtraction facts for each number up to 20.	Derive doubles of whole numbers to 20, corresponding halves. Derive near doubles. Recall pairs of multiples of 100 that make 1000. Recognise odd/even numbers to 100. Recall multiplication facts in ×2, ×5 and ×10 tables and derive division facts. Recall multiplication facts up to 5 × 5.

Unit	Teacher's page	Pupil page	Topic	Objectives children will be taught
8	17	20–21	Counting, properties of numbers and number sequences Reasoning about numbers	Count larger collections by grouping them in tens then other numbers. Count on/back in 10s/100s, starting from any two-/three-digit number. Count on or back in twos, starting from any two-digit number and recognise odd and even numbers to at least 100. Solve number puzzles. Explain methods and reading orally and in writing.
9	18	22–23	Understanding × and ÷	Understand multiplication as repeated addition and as an array. Read and begin to write related vocabulary. Recognise that multiplication can be done in any order.
10	19	24–25	Mental calculation strategies (× and ÷) Money and 'real life' problems Making decisions, checking results	To multiply by 10/100, shift the digits one/two places to the left. Choose an appropriate number operation and calculation method to solve word problems involving money and 'real life'. Explain and record method informally. Check multiplication in a different order.
11	20	26–27	Fractions	Recognise unit fractions ½, ⅓, ¼, ⅕, ⅒ and use them to find fractions of shapes and numbers. Begin to recognise fractions that are several parts of a whole: ⅔, ¾, $\frac{3}{10}$.
12	21	28–29	Understanding + and – Mental calculation strategies (+ and –) Time, including problems Making decisions, checking results	Understand that subtraction is the inverse of addition. Say a subtraction statement equivalent to an addition statement and vice versa. Find a small difference by counting up from the smaller number. Read and begin to write the vocabulary related to time. Use units of time and relationship between them. Choose appropriate number operations and calculation methods to solve word problems. Explain and record method. Check subtraction with addition.
13	22	30–31	Handling data	Solve a given problem by organising and interpreting data in frequency tables, and in pictograms with the symbol representing two units.
14	23	32–33	Assess and review	

Teaching plan for Term 2

EVERY DAY: Practise and develop oral and mental skills (e.g. counting, mental strategies, rapid recall of +, –, × and ÷ facts)

Read and write whole numbers up to 1000. Count on/back in 10s, 100s from any two-/three-digit number. State subtraction fact corresponding to addition fact, and vice versa. Recall addition and subtraction facts for each number up to 20. Recall pairs of multiples of 100 with a total of 1000.	Order a set of three-digit numbers. Derive doubles of whole numbers to 20, corresponding halves. Derive near doubles. Count on or back in twos. Recognise odd/even numbers to 100. Recall multiplication facts in ×2, ×5 and ×10 tables and derive division facts.

Unit	Teacher's page	Pupil page	Topic	Objectives children will be taught
1	26	36–37	Place value, ordering, estimating, rounding Reading numbers from scales	Read and write the vocabulary of comparing and ordering numbers, including ordinal numbers to 100. Compare two three-digit numbers and say which is more or less. Read and begin to write the vocabulary of approximation. Round any two-digit number to nearest 10. Read scales and dials.
2–3	27–28	38–41	Understanding + and – Mental calculation strategies (+ and –)	Add three then four single-digit numbers mentally. Add three or four small numbers by putting the largest number first and/or finding pairs that total 10. Partition into 5 and a bit to add 6, 7 or 8.
4	29	42–43	Money and 'real life' problems Making decisions, checking results	Choose appropriate number operations and calculation methods to solve money or 'real life' word problems with one or more steps. Explain and record method. Check with an equivalent calculation.
5	30	44–45	Shape and space Reasoning about shapes	Make and describe shapes and patterns. Relate solid shapes to pictures of them. Read and begin to write the vocabulary of direction. Make and use right-angled turns, and use the four compass points. Solve shape problems or puzzles. Explain reasoning and methods.
6	31	46–47	Measures, and time, including problems	Read time to 5 minutes on analogue and 12-hour digital clocks (e.g. 9:40). Read and begin to write the vocabulary related to mass. Measure and compare using kilograms and grams, and know the relationship between them. Suggest suitable units and equipment to estimate or measure mass. Read scales. Record measurements using mixed units, or to the nearest whole/half unit (e.g. 3.5 kg). Choose appropriate number operations and calculation methods to solve measurement word problems with one or more steps. Explain and record method.
7	32	48–49	Assess and review	

Read and write whole numbers up to 1000. Count on or back in 10s, 100s from any two-/three-digit number. State subtraction fact corresponding to addition fact, and vice versa. Derive doubles of whole numbers to 20, corresponding halves. Derive doubles of multiples of 5 to 50. Recall addition and subtraction facts for each number up to 20.	Recall pairs of multiples of 100 with a total of 1000. Recall pairs of multiples of 5 with a total of 100. Recall multiplication facts in ×2, ×5, ×10 tables and derive division facts. Recall multiplication facts in ×3 table. Order a set of three-digit numbers.

Unit	Teacher's page	Pupil page	Topic	Objectives children will be taught
8	33	50–51	Counting, properties of numbers and number sequences Reasoning about numbers	Count on in steps of 3 or 4 or 5 from any small number to at least 50 and back again. Create and describe simple number sequences. Investigate general statements about familiar numbers, and give examples that match them. Solve number puzzles. Explain methods and reasoning orally and in writing.
9–10	34–35	52–55	Understanding + and – Mental calculation strategies (+ and –) Understanding × and ÷ Mental calculation strategies (× and ÷) Money and 'real life' problems Making decisions, checking results	Add three two-digit numbers using apparatus or informal methods. Partition into tens and units and recombine. Understand division as grouping or sharing. Read and begin to write the related vocabulary. Recognise division is inverse of multiplication. Use doubling and halving, starting from known facts. Say or write division statement corresponding to multiplication statement. Choose appropriate number operations and calculation methods to solve money or 'real life' word problems with two steps. Explain and record method. Check results, e.g. check division by multiplication, halving by doubling.
11	36	56–57	Fractions	Begin to recognise simple equivalent fractions, e.g. $\frac{5}{10}$ is equivalent to $\frac{1}{2}$, $\frac{5}{5}$ to 1 whole.
12	37	58–59	Handling data	Solve a given problem by organising and interpreting data in bar charts – intervals labelled in ones then twos.
13	38	60–61	Assess and review	

Teaching plan for Term 3

EVERY DAY: Practise and develop oral and mental skills (e.g. counting, mental strategies, rapid recall of +, –, × and ÷ facts)	
Read and write whole numbers up to 1000. Order a set of three-digit numbers. Count on/back in 10s, 100s from any two-/three-digit number. State subtraction fact corresponding to addition fact, and vice versa. Derive doubles of multiples of 5 to 50, corresponding halves. Derive doubles of multiples of 50 to 500. Add/subtract 9, 19, 29… and 11, 21, 31…	Recall addition and subtraction facts for each number up to 20. Recall pairs of multiples of 100 with a total of 1000. Recall pairs of multiples of 5 with a total of 100. Recall multiplication facts in ×2, ×5 and ×10 tables and derive division facts. Count in threes from and back to zero. Recall multiplication facts in ×3 table and begin to derive division facts.

Unit	Teacher's page	Pupil page	Topic	Objectives children will be taught
1	40	64–65	Place value, ordering, estimating, rounding Reading numbers from scales	Compare two three-digit numbers, say which is more or less and give a number that lies between them. Round any three-digit number to the nearest 100. Order a set of whole numbers to 1000; position them on a number line. Identify unlabelled divisions on a number line or measuring scale.
2	41	66–67	Understanding + and – Mental calculation strategies (+ and –)	Extend understanding of addition and subtraction. Add several small numbers. Add or subtract a near multiple of 10 to a two-digit number, by adding or subtracting the nearest multiple of 10, and adjusting. Use patterns of similar calculations.
3	42	68–69	Money and 'real life' problems Making decisions, checking results	Choose appropriate number operations and calculation methods to solve money or 'real life' word problems with one or two steps. Explain and record method. Check results. Use informal pencil and paper methods to support,
4	43	70–71	Pencil and paper procedures	record or explain TU + TU, HTU + TU and HTU + HTU.
5	44	72–73	Measures, including problems	Read and begin to write the vocabulary related to capacity. Measure and compare using *litres* and *millilitres*, and know the relationship between them. Suggest suitable units and equipment to estimate or measure capacity. Read scales. Record measurements using mixed units, or to the nearest whole/half unit (e.g. 3.5 litres). Choose appropriate number operations and calculation methods to solve measurement word problems with one or more steps. Explain and record method.
6	45	74–75	Shape and space Reasoning about shapes	Identify and sketch lines of symmetry, recognise shapes with no line of symmetry. Sketch reflection of simple shape in a mirror. Read and begin to write the vocabulary of position, direction and movement. Recognise that a straight line is two right angles. Compare angles with a right angle, saying whether they are more or less. Investigate general statements about shapes, and suggest examples to match them. Explain reasoning.
7	46	76–77	Assess and review	

Read and write whole numbers up to 1000. Count on/back in 10s, 100s from any two-/three-digit number. Derive doubles of multiples of 5 to 50, corresponding halves. Derive doubles of multiples of 50 to 500, corresponding halves. Round any three-digit number to the nearest 100. Order a set of three-digit numbers. Add/subtract 9, 19, 29… and 11, 21, 31…	Recall addition and subtraction facts for each number up to 20. Recall pairs of multiples of 100 with a total of 1000. Recall pairs of multiples of 5 with a total of 100. Recall multiplication facts in ×2, ×5, ×10 tables and derive division facts. Recall multiplication facts in the ×3 table, then in ×4 table. Begin to derive division facts in the ×3 and ×4 tables. State division fact corresponding to a multiplication fact.

Unit	Teacher's page	Pupil page	Topic	Objectives children will be taught
8	47	78–79	Counting, properties of numbers and number sequences Reasoning about numbers	Recognise two-digit and three-digit multiples of 2, 5 and 10 and three-digit multiples of 50 and 100. Solve number puzzles. Explain methods and reasoning orally and in writing.
9	48	80–81	Understanding × and ÷ Mental calculation strategies (× and ÷)	Begin to find remainders after division. Round up or down after division. Use known facts and place value to multiply and divide mentally.
10	49	82–83	Money and 'real life' problems Making decisions, checking results	Choose appropriate number operations and calculation methods to solve money or 'real life' word problems with one or two steps. Explain and record method. Check results.
11	50	84–85	Fractions	Compare two familiar fractions. Know that ½ lies between ¼ and ¾. Estimate a simple fraction (proportion) of a shape.
12	51	86–87	Understanding + and – Mental calculation strategies (+ and –) Pencil and paper procedures Time, including problems Making decisions, checking results	Add using pencil and paper methods. Use known number facts and place value to add/subtract mentally. Use informal pencil and paper methods to support, record or explain TU – TU and HTU – TU. Use a calendar. Choose appropriate number operations and calculation methods to solve time word problems with one or two steps. Explain and record methods. Check results.
13	52	88–89	Handling data	Solve a given problem by organising and interpreting data in Venn and Carroll diagrams – one criterion.
14	53	90–91		Assess and review

Use pupil pages 4 and 5 to talk about some activities which have been covered in the previous term's work.

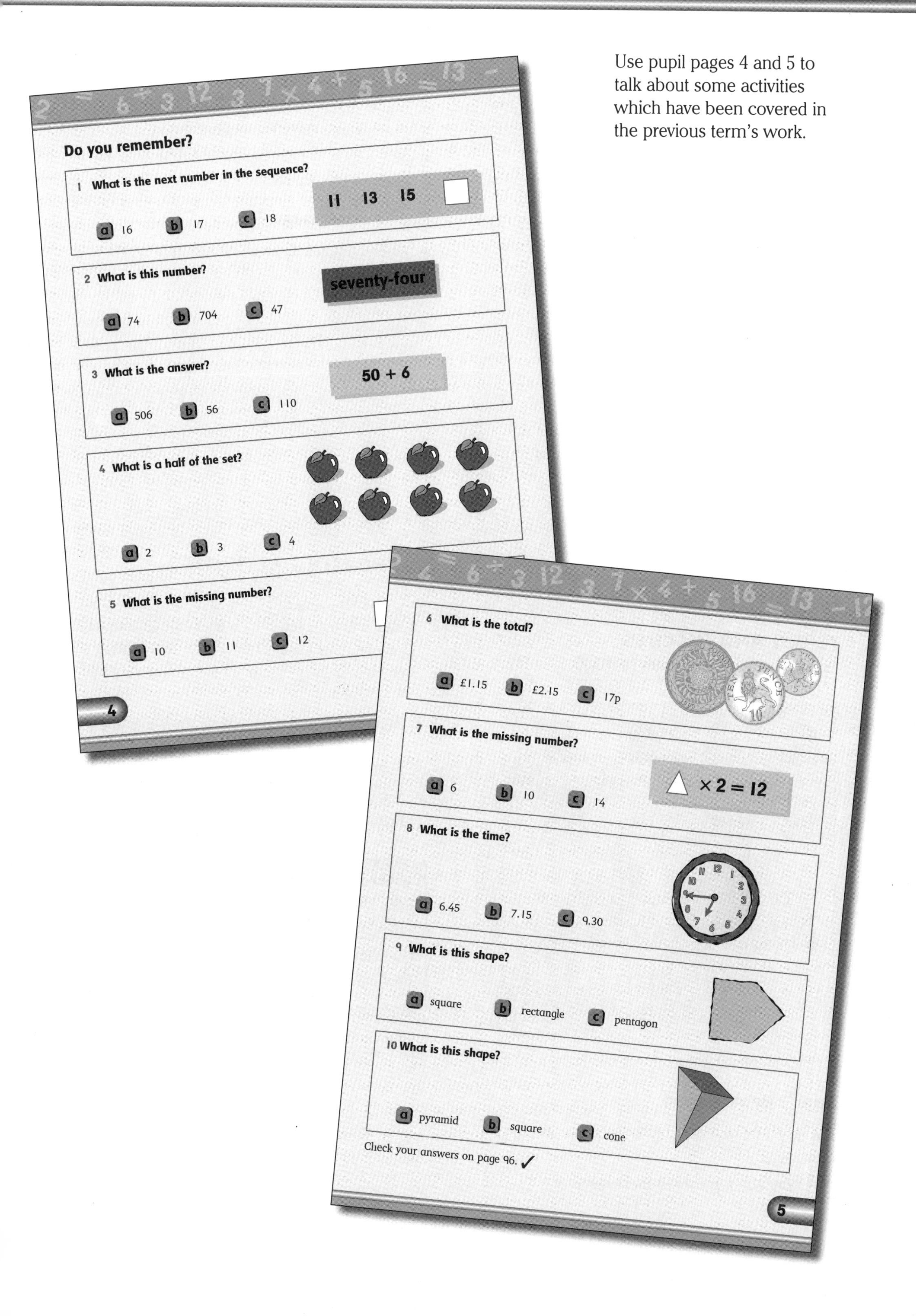

Do you remember?

1 What is the next number in the sequence?

11 13 15 □

a 16 b 17 c 18

2 What is this number?

seventy-four

a 74 b 704 c 47

3 What is the answer?

50 + 6

a 506 b 56 c 110

4 What is a half of the set?

a 2 b 3 c 4

5 What is the missing number?

a 10 b 11 c 12

4

6 What is the total?

a £1.15 b £2.15 c 17p

7 What is the missing number?

△ × 2 = 12

a 6 b 10 c 14

8 What is the time?

a 6.45 b 7.15 c 9.30

9 What is this shape?

a square b rectangle c pentagon

10 What is this shape?

a pyramid b square c cone

Check your answers on page 96. ✓

5

Place value

MENTAL MATHS

- Pupils should count on and back in tens in unison in time to a rhythm. This can be set up by clapping patterns or to a swinging pendulum. Choose an appropriate number range.
- Ask questions about addition and subtraction facts to 10. Pupils respond by holding up number cards to indicate their response. Include open and closed questions and a range of number language.
- Ask questions about adding and subtracting 1 and 10 with a range of numbers. Ideally this should be as a 'show me' activity with apparatus such as digit cards, fan numbers, digit flips or number generators.
- Check that pupils can add and subtract a single digit to and from a range of numbers without bridging a tens number.

TEACH AND DISCUSS

Learning about numbers to 1000

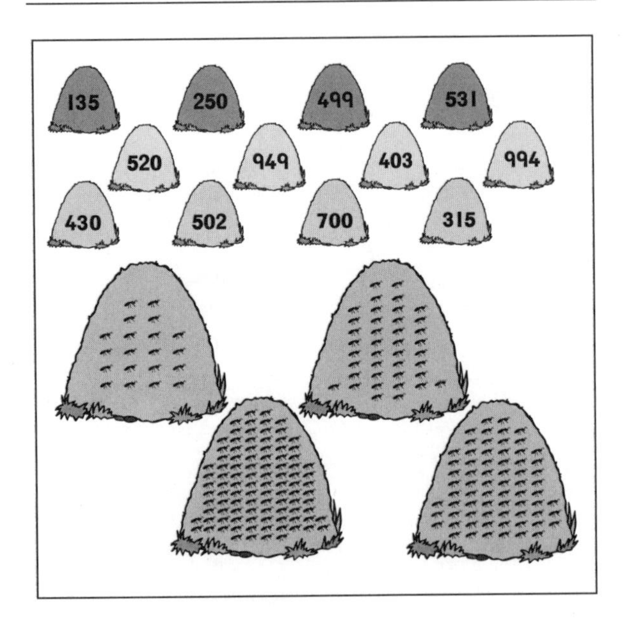

Pupil's Book: page 6

Pupils cover one or more numbers with counters.

- *Cover the largest/smallest number.*
- *Cover all numbers between 500 and 600.*
- *Cover the numbers that have the digit 3 in the tens position.*
- *Cover up the number: four hundred and three, three hundred and fifteen, …*
- Ask pupils to estimate how many ants are in each of the ant hills.

Pupil's Book: page 7

- Check that each pupil can read and write whole numbers to 1000. Ask them to write each of the numbers in words.
- Discuss what each division on the number line stands for. Query the value of the half-way position.
- Query what each division on the measuring jugs represents.

Challenge

Pupils should use actual digit cards as part of the activity. Use other sets of three digits.

SUPPORTING ACTIVITIES

- Use a strip of card on which is threaded an elastic band. Tell pupils that one end of the strip is 0 and the other is 100. Ask them to move the band to show the position of: 40, 80, 50, 75, …
- Repeat the previous activity, naming the ends 0 and 1000. Pupils show the positions of numbers such as 300, 700, 400, 250, …
- See further activities in *Numeracy Activity Book Year 3* pages 12–17.

Vocabulary
place value, digits, value, worth, relationship
number words – tens, hundreds, thousands, between, after, before
estimate, approximate, approximately, nearly, about, more, less

Addition and subtraction

MENTAL MATHS

- Pupils should count on and back in tens and hundreds from 2-digit and 3-digit numbers, for example '10 more than' numbers can ripple round the class from one pupil to the next.
- Ask questions about addition and subtraction facts of numbers within 10. Pupils respond by holding up number cards to indicate their response. Include open and closed questions and a range of number language.
- Ask questions about multiplication and division table facts for twos. Pupils respond by holding up number cards to indicate their response. Include open and closed questions and a range of number language.
- Check that pupils can multiply a single-digit number by 1, 10 or 100.

TEACH AND DISCUSS

Using facts about adding and subtracting

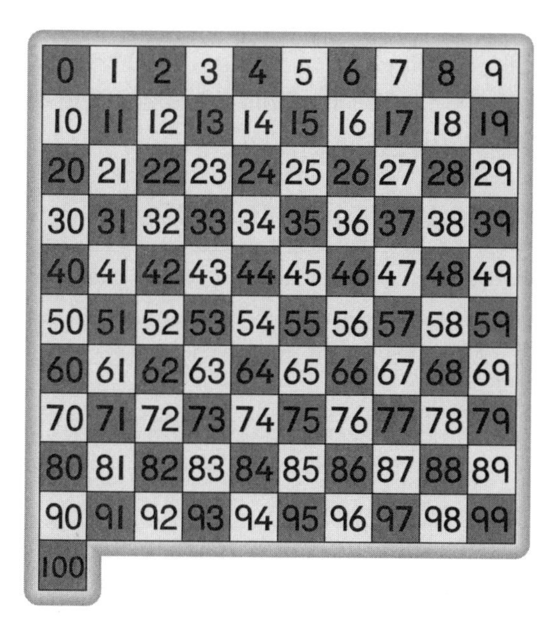

Pupil's Book: page 8

Each pupil will need counters to cover some of the numbers on the grid.

- Discuss adding and subtracting 1 and 10 with numbers on the grid.
- Extend to adding and subtracting 9 with a range of numbers, checking that pupils do not move their counters in ones.
- Tell pupils to cover a pair of stated multiples of 10, such as 30 and 70. Ask for the total and difference between the covered numbers.
- Tell pupils to cover a stated 2-digit number such as 48. Ask for the result of adding a small number such as 6 to the number. Involve pupils in numbers that bridge a tens number.
- Check that pupils know the multiples of 5, including those beyond 50. They should use the grid to help them answer the investigations at the bottom of the page.

Pupil's Book: page 9

- Discuss strategies for addition of numbers, such as putting the larger number first and looking for pairs that total 10, or a multiple of 10.
- Check that pupils know that an addition undoes a subtraction and vice versa.

Challenge

Number cards should be used. Encourage looking for alternative solutions. Pupils should record their results.

SUPPORTING ACTIVITIES

- Any games, investigations, problems that involve pupils in using addition and subtraction facts.
- See further activities in *Numeracy Activity Book Year 3* pages 22–35.
- Discuss doubles and near doubles, checking that pupils can identify near doubles.

Vocabulary
add, addition, total, plus, sum, subtract, subtraction, take away, minus, difference, answer, result, equals, calculation
multiple, tens, fives, odd, even, double, tens boundary, hundreds boundary
strategy, method, another way, choose, decide, explain

Money and problems

MENTAL MATHS

- Pupils should add and subtract 1, 10 and 100 with a range of numbers. Divide pupils into two groups to play 'ping pong'. Select a pupil from one group to give a starting number and a pupil from the other group to add 1, 10 or 100 to that number. Numbers 'ping pong' between the two groups having had 1, 10 or 100 added to them.
- Ask questions about number pairs that make 20. Pupils respond by holding up number cards to indicate their response.
- Ask questions about multiplication and division table facts for tens. Pupils respond by holding up number cards to indicate their response. Include open and closed questions and a range of number language.
- Check that pupils can multiply a single-digit number by 1, 10 or 100.

TEACH AND DISCUSS

Money and solving problems

Pupil's Book: page 10

- Discuss the two price lists, comparing the prices.
- Ask for the change received from £1 and £2 coins for nominated items from the lists.
- Talk about strategies for adding pairs of items, for example one costing 99p and the other 55p.
- Talk about the most expensive and least expensive items.
- Discuss the value of coins, extending to the different denomination notes that we use.
- Explain how shopkeepers make up one amount to the next when giving change, rather than doing a take away sum.
- Tell pupils to choose three items and to make a list. They should total the cost of the list.
- Explain about the £/p notation, such as £2.05.

Pupil's Book: page 11

- Check that pupils can recognise all coins and notes.
- Some pupils may require coins to help with the calculations. Check that pupils are using shopkeeper methods for finding how much change is needed. Discuss the informal methods of recording that pupils employ.
- Decide whether calculators can be used to check the calculations. This will get pupils inputting and reading money notation in a different way from the written notation.

Challenge

Encourage alternative solutions to the problem. Pupils should record and check that their selection of books is within the £5 limit. Discuss checking by adding up in a different order.

SUPPORTING ACTIVITIES

See further activities in *Numeracy Activity Book Year 3:*

- for simple addition problems pages 18, 25, 28, 36
- for simple subtraction problems pages 46, 48, 51
- for notation problems page 91.

Vocabulary
total, add, altogether, take away, more than, less than, double, difference, multiply
money, coins, note, value, amount, total, change, price, cheap, dear, expensive, penny, pence, pound, pay, buy, sell, spend
compare, count, match, total, explain, work out, check, another way, record, list

Measures

MENTAL MATHS

- Talk about doubling and halving whole numbers up to 15. Start with the even numbers then focus on the odd numbers. A number line can help many pupils.
- Ask questions about number pairs that total 20. Pupils respond by holding up number cards to indicate their response.
- Ask questions about multiplication and division table facts for 5. Pupils respond by holding up number cards to indicate their response. Include open and closed questions and a range of number language.
- Check that pupils can mentally add any 2-digit number to a multiple of 100, for example 34 + 600.

TEACH AND DISCUSS

Measuring units

Pupil's Book: page 12

- Talk about what is being measured in each picture on the pupil page – temperature, capacity, time, speed, weight, length.
- Focus on the divisions of each 'instrument' and talk about the reading they would show.
- Explain how sometimes the reading is not exactly on a division mark. Query what we have to do when this happens.
- Talk about the readings shown on the page, asking questions such as: *Are the weights heavy or light? Is there a lot of water in the measuring jug? Enough to fill a cup? Is the pencil a long or short one? What do you think the numbers on the speedo/odometer show?*
- The questions on the page can be answered orally or be recorded.

Pupil's Book: page 13

- Check that pupils can read a clock face to 5-minute intervals. Talk about a.m. and p.m. times.
- Discuss the abbreviations we use when measuring.
- Talk about the appropriateness and otherwise of different units for measuring activities.

Challenge

- Encourage finding several examples of each prefix. Pupils should also think about other non-measuring words that begin with these prefixes. A dictionary should help.

SUPPORTING ACTIVITIES

- See further activities in *Numeracy Activity Book Year 3* pages 6–11.
- Talk about some of the imperial units that pupils might meet, such as inches.
- Discuss some historical facts about measurements, such as Egyptian cubits and Roman paces.

Vocabulary
measure, size, weigh, fill, length, weight, capacity, time, speed, balance, scales, weights, tape measure, metre stick, ruler, container
division, marks, nearly, about, approximately, roughly, close to, just over, just under, just before, just after, half-way, full, empty, compare
kilometre, mile, metre, centimetre, kilogram, gram, litre, millilitre, half litre, minute, hour, a.m., p.m.

Length

MENTAL MATHS

- Talk about doubling and halving whole numbers up to 15. Start with the even numbers then focus on the odd numbers. A number line can help many pupils.
- Ask pupils to add and subtract 1, 10 and 100 with a range of numbers. Include multiplying a single digit by 1, 10 and 100. Ideally these should be 'show me' activities with apparatus such as place value arrow cards, fan numbers, digit flips, number generators.
- Ask questions about multiplication and division table facts for 5. Pupils respond by holding up number cards to indicate their response. Include open and closed questions and a range of number language.
- Check that pupils can mentally add any 2-digit number to a multiple of 100, for example 87 + 700.

TEACH AND DISCUSS

Measuring lengths

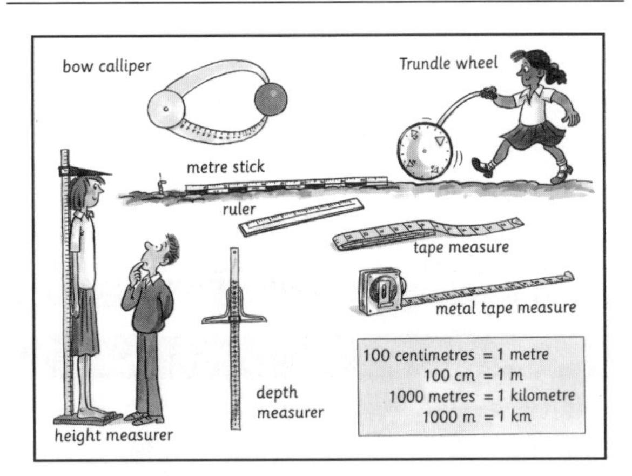

Pupil's Book: page 14

- Have a selection of different measuring instruments such as depth gauges, callipers, tapes, rulers. Talk about what they would be used for and what they would measure: *Would you use a trundle wheel to measure the length of this line? What would you use to measure round a tree?*
- Discuss the measuring units used on these instruments: *Would you find metres on your personal ruler?*
- Talk about the relationship between kilometres, metres and centimetres. Many of the rulers that pupils have access to have millimetres marked on them. Decide whether to make reference to these.
- Explain the decimal notation for m and cm and the equivalent mixed-unit notation, for example 2 m 25 cm = 2.25 m.
- Talk about measurement in general, making use of comparative language such as closest, furthest, nearest, far away, close to, nearby.

Pupil's Book: page 15

- Check that pupils can use a ruler to measure to the nearest half centimetre.
- Check that pupils know how many centimetres are in a metre and can use the decimal notation for recording metres and centimetres.

Challenge

Encourage estimation before measuring, reassuring pupils that estimation is rarely 'spot on', especially when measuring perimeters and circumferences.

SUPPORTING ACTIVITIES

- See further activities in *Numeracy Activity Book Year 3* page 19.
- Any practical activities that involve pupils in comparing and measuring lengths and distances. Include words such as width, depth, length, height, distance, thickness. Refer to measuring to the nearest m/cm, and to the nearest half cm/m.
- Talk about estimating the lengths and distances of items in and around the classroom.

Vocabulary
measure, length, width, height, depth, long, short, tall, high, wide, deep, thick, distance apart, distance to, distance between, distance from
metre stick, ruler, tape measure, metre, centimetre, kilometre, mile, division, marks, nearly, about, approximately, roughly, close to, just over, just under, just before, just after, half-way
closest, furthest, nearest, far away, close to, nearby, highest, lowest, shortest, longest

Shape and space

MENTAL MATHS

- Talk about time, checking that pupils can tell the time to 5-minute intervals. Refer to months, days and special events, focusing on how dates are said.
- Pupils should add and subtract 1, 10 and 100 with a range of numbers. Ideally this should be as a 'show me' activity with apparatus such as place value arrow cards, fan numbers, digit flips, number generators.
- Ask questions about multiplication and division table facts for 2, 5 and 10. Pupils respond by holding up number cards to indicate their response. Include open and closed questions and a range of number language.
- Check that pupils can mentally add any 2-digit number to a multiple of 100, for example 34 + 600.

TEACH AND DISCUSS
Shapes and space

Pupil's Book: page 16

Pupils place a counter on the map to indicate different positions.

- Involve pupils in placing a counter on a nominated square and in describing that position in relation to other places on the map.
- Have pupils follow a mystery journey with their counter. Give verbal instructions that will take them from one position to another, asking: *Where have we ended up?*
- Ask for instructions on how to move from one place to another. Discuss words that help this, such as up, down, left, right, north, south, east, west.
- Explain about making a diagonal move and what moving diagonally means.

Pupil's Book: page 17

- Talk about quarter turns and right angles, ensuring that pupils can recognise right angles in shapes. Allow the use of a 'right angle checker'.
- Discuss prisms and non-prisms.
- Check that pupils know that quadrilaterals are any 4-sided shape and that shapes such as squares and rectangles are special types of quadrilaterals.
- Ask how shapes can be checked for lines of symmetry such as by folding or by using a mirror.

Challenge

Pupils should use shapes to create symmetrical patterns of triangles. This can be extended to making computer patterns with triangles.

SUPPORTING ACTIVITIES

- Have pupils make turns, half turns and quarter turns making reference to clockwise, anticlockwise and the points of the compass.
- Use Roamer and Logo programs to set simple problems involving turns and directions.
- Sort prisms using language such as triangular, pentagonal, octagonal and hexagonal. Simple Venn and Carroll diagrams are excellent for this. Note that cubes and cuboids are special examples of prisms.
- Play 'pass the parcel' with a shape. Each pupil gives a different fact about the shape as it passes from pupil to pupil. Prompt words such as faces, edge, vertices, sides, corners, symmetry.

Vocabulary
position, left, right, north, south, east, west, up, down, diagonally, over, under, beside, between, side, above, below, underneath, apart, map, plan, row, column, compass point, horizontal, vertical
prism, hemisphere, cube, cuboid, pyramid, cone, cylinder, triangular, rectangular, hexagonal, pentagonal, octagonal, quadrilateral
right angled, right angle, turn, quarter turn, half turn, whole turn, symmetrical, reflection, line of symmetry, fold, match

Review

MENTAL MATHS

- Ask questions about number pairs that total 20. Pupils respond by holding up number cards to indicate their response.
- Ask pupils to add and subtract 1, 10 and 100 with a range of numbers. Include multiplying a single digit by 1, 10 and 100. Ideally these should be 'show me' activities with apparatus such as place value arrow cards, fan numbers, digit flips, number generators.
- Ask questions about multiplication and division table facts for 2, 5 and 10. Pupils respond by holding up number cards to indicate their response. Include open and closed questions and a range of number language.
- Check that pupils can mentally add any 2-digit number to a multiple of 100, for example 34 + 600.

Pupil's Book: pages 18 and 19

The pupil pages give the opportunity to assess and review:

- place value to about 1000
- estimation skills for numbers on a number line
- addition and subtraction involving bridging 20
- totalling coins and calculating change
- telling the time
- measuring lines
- equivalence of metres and centimetres
- recognition of 3D shapes
- right angles and quadrilaterals.

Other areas for discussion should include:

Say, read and use number names to 1000

Check all pupils can say the number names of numbers to at least one thousand.

Estimation skills

Check pupils understand estimation of quantity and can make sensible estimations of up to 100 objects.

Understanding addition

Check pupils know that addition can be done in any order, and that they know the plus and equals symbols.

Understanding subtraction

Check pupils understand that subtraction can be taking away or difference. They should also know the minus symbol.

Key vocabulary
Counting and place value *hundreds, relationship, one hundred more, one hundred less, approximate, approximately*
Measuring *divisions, approximately, distance apart, ...between, ...to, ...from, kilometre, mile*
Adding and subtracting *add, subtract, plus, minus, total, equals, operation, sign*
Shape *hemisphere, prism, quadrilateral, pentagonal, hexagonal, octagonal, right angled*
Position and direction *map, plan, row, column, compass point, north, south, east, west, horizontal, vertical, diagonal, angle*
Time *a.m., p.m.*

Counting

MENTAL MATHS

- Ask questions about addition and subtraction facts within 20. Include pupils responding by holding up number cards to indicate their answers.
- Ask questions about adding and subtracting 10 and 100 with a range of numbers. Ideally these should be 'show me' activities with apparatus such as place value arrow cards, fan numbers, digit flips, number generators.
- Check that pupils can link addition facts to subtraction facts and vice versa. Ask for different number sentences based on the same number trio, such as 13, 7, 6.
- Involve pupils in subtracting a single digit from a multiple of 100, for example 600 – 8.

TEACH AND DISCUSS

Counting and properties of numbers

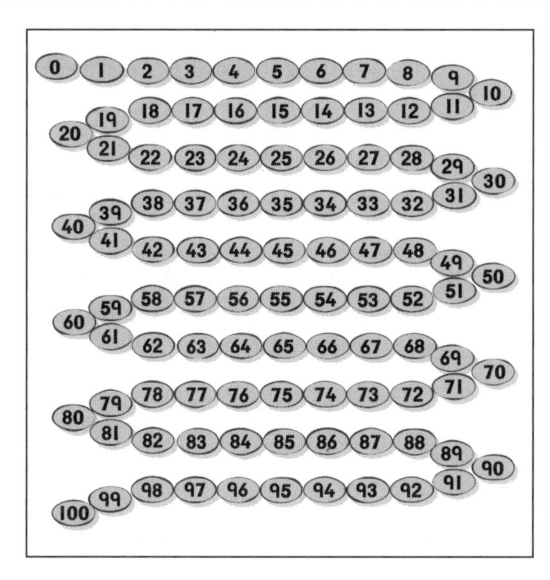

Pupil's Book: page 20

Pupils cover numbers on the track with counters.

- *Cover these numbers: 76, 55, 92, …*
- *Cover the number: after 36, before 99, between 62 and 64, …*
- *Cover 10 more than: 12, 51, 75, …*
- *Cover an odd number that is greater than 75.*
- *Cover an even number that is between 70 and 90.*
- Involve pupils in counting on and back in tens and hundreds starting from any 2-digit or 3-digit number.
- Involve pupils in counting on and back in twos starting from any 2-digit number.

Pupil's Book: page 21

- Check that pupils can count in tens and ones.
- Talk about the missing number sequences.
- Talk about odd, even and multiples.

Challenge

Check that pupils do not rely upon just one example to prove or disprove the statement. Try to get them to explain their conclusion.

SUPPORTING ACTIVITIES

- Use place value arrow cards to create 2-digit and 3-digit numbers. Ask for numbers that are 10 more/less and 100 more/less than a range of numbers.
- Use place value apparatus such as Dienes to model large numbers; this shows grouping in tens, hundreds and thousands.
- See further activities in *Numeracy Activity Book Year 3* pages 12–16.

Vocabulary
place value, digit, worth, value, relationship, hundreds
order, sequence, pattern, what next?, continue, carry on, before, after, between, next to
odd, even, multiple

Multiplication tables

MENTAL MATHS

- Talk about doubling and halving whole numbers up to 20. Start with the even numbers then focus on the odd numbers. A number line can help many pupils.
- Ask pupils about odd and even numbers to 100.
- Ask questions about multiplication and division table facts for 2, 5 and 10. Pupils respond by holding up number cards to indicate their response. Include open and closed questions and a range of number language.
- Involve pupils in subtracting a single digit from a multiple of 100, for example 400 – 7.

TEACH AND DISCUSS

Multiplication tables for 2, 3, 4, 5 and 10

Pupil's Book: page 22

- Talk about arrays and how they show multiplication facts, for example an array of 2 cubes by 4 cubes shows 2×4 or 4×2 and the answer of 8. Arrays also show the repeated addition aspect of multiplication.
- Query which multiplication facts each of the arrays shows. Check that pupils realise that multiplication is commutative, for example that $2 \times 4 = 4 \times 2$.
- Explain the multiplication table on the page and talk how about it can be used to find multiplication or division facts for 2, 3, 4, 5 and 10.

Pupil's Book: page 23

- Pupils should answer as many of the facts as they can without using the multiplication table to help them.
- The word problems can be answered verbally or be written responses.

Challenge

Encourage pupils to find several possible solutions for each open equation. Prompt a systematic approach rather than random trial and error.

SUPPORTING ACTIVITIES

- See further activities in *Numeracy Activity Book Year 3* pages 62–81.
- Involve pupils in any multiplication and division activities that encourage rapid recall of the multiplication facts. These include table bingo, multiplication dominoes, table snap, fizz-buzz, etc.
- Discuss multiplying numbers by 10 and discuss the pattern. Extend this to multiplying by 100.

Vocabulary
product, times, multiply, multiple, groups of, repeated addition, double array, row, column
halve, divide, share, group, lots of
question, answer, result, how?, method, explain, what is missing?, equation

Multiplication problems

MENTAL MATHS

- Talk about doubling and halving whole numbers up to 20. Extend to talking about near doubles and quick methods of totalling these.
- Question quick recall of addition and subtraction facts of numbers within 20. Include the relationship between the two operations – how an addition is the opposite of subtraction.
- Talk about multiples of 100 that total 1000, for example 600 and 400.
- Involve pupils in finding doubles of multiples of 5 to 50, for example double 35.

TEACH AND DISCUSS

Using multiplication facts to answer problems

Pupil's Book: page 24

- Talk about the individual prices of the objects and ask for simple totals of pairs of items. Extend to totalling three items.
- Ask for the difference between individual prices – how much more one item is than another.
- Query multiple purchases of the same item and how knowing tables can help in this.
- Ask questions that involve pupils in finding change from different denomination notes. Ensure that these questions involve several stages, such as totalling before finding the change.

Pupil's Book: page 25

- Discuss multiplying three numbers together and how the choice of the first multiplication can make life easier.
- Ensure that pupils can mentally multiply any 2-digit number by 10.
- Talk about the effect of doubling then doubling again. Check that pupils know that doubling can be times 2 or adding the same number twice.

Challenge

Pupils should use each set of three numbers to create several different multiplication and division sums such as $4 \times 6 = 24$ and $24 \div 6 = 4$. Discuss multiplying in a different order and the effect on the answer.

SUPPORTING ACTIVITIES

- See further activities in *Numeracy Activity Book Year 3* pages 62–81.
- Involve pupils in any multiplication and division activities that encourage rapid recall of the multiplication facts. These include table bingo, multiplication dominoes, table snap, fizz-buzz, etc.
- Give multiplication facts as word problems for pupils to answer.
- Write a multiplication fact on the board. Ask pupils for a word problem to match the sum.

Vocabulary
multiplication, product, times, multiply, multiple, groups of, repeated addition, double, array, row, column
division, halve, divide, share, group, lots of
question, answer, result, how?, method, explain, what is missing?, equation

Fractions

MENTAL MATHS

- Ask questions about multiplication of numbers by 10, and multiplication facts to 5×5.
- Involve pupils in using counting skills to answer mental calculations with 'large numbers'. Include: finding close differences for numbers such as 134 and 138; adding and subtracting a small number and a large number, such as 345 + 4 and 568 – 5; adding and subtracting 10 and 100 from a range of numbers.
- Explain how to make up a number to the next multiple of 10. For example: *What must be added to 124 to make 130?*
- Involve pupils in finding doubles of multiples of 5 to 50, for example double 35.

TEACH AND DISCUSS

Finding fractions of shapes and quantities

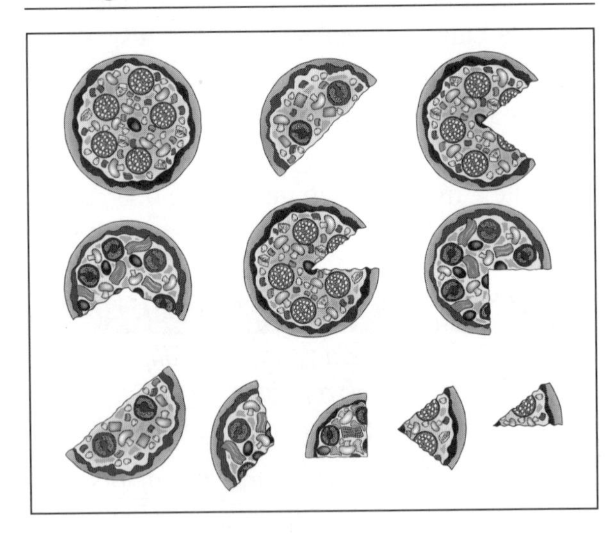

Pupil's Book: page 26

- Talk about the various fractions shown on the page.
- Explain how the fractional parts need to be the same size, for example the difference between cutting into three parts and cutting into thirds.
- Discuss fractions that have a numerator greater than 1.
- Challenge pupils with thinking about when two halves need not be the same. For example, half a small cake is not the same as half a large cake.

Pupil's Book: page 27

- Pupils may need to use counters to help find fraction parts of quantity.
- Talk about the link between fractions of quantity and division, for example half is the same as ÷2.

Challenge

Pupils should work co-operatively to make a set of models to match the criteria. Discuss how many of each colour create each model.

SUPPORTING ACTIVITIES

- Pupils use a strip of card onto which is threaded an elastic band. They slide the band along the strip to show half, quarter and three-quarters.
- See further activities in *Numeracy Activity Book Year 3* pages 82–87.

Vocabulary
fraction, part, equal parts, divide, whole
half, halves, quarter, three-quarters, third, two-thirds, tenth
think, remember, look at, point to, show me, find, choose, decide, make, build, tell me, discuss, talk about

Subtraction and time

MENTAL MATHS

- Ask questions about pairs of multiples of 100 that make 1000, for example 600 + 400.
- Ask questions about adding and subtracting 10 and 100 with a range of numbers. Extend to multiplying by 10. Ideally these should be 'show me' activities with apparatus such as place value arrow cards, fan numbers, digit flips, number generators.
- Explain how to make up a number to the next multiple of 10, for example: *What must be added to 56 to make 60?* Extend to making a range of 2-digit numbers up to 100.
- Involve pupils in making up a 3-digit multiples of 10 up to the next highest multiple of 100, such as making up 730 to 800.

TEACH AND DISCUSS

Subtraction facts and time facts

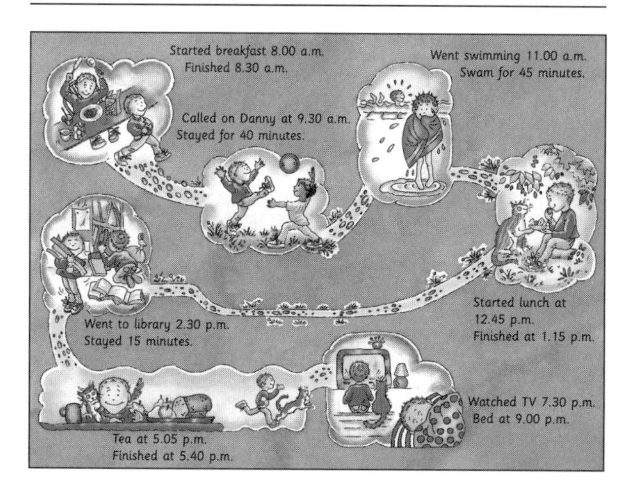

Pupil's Book: page 28

- Discuss morning times and afternoon times, referring to a.m. and p.m.
- Talk about the typical sequence of daily events and when they are most likely to occur.
- Look at the picture-strip story on the page. Ask how long each event lasted. Also ask when each started and ended.
- Explain how to work out how long it is from times such as 3.25 to the next hour.
- Check that pupils know the relationship between common units of time, such as days/week, hours/minutes, minutes/seconds.

Pupil's Book: page 29

- Check that pupils know what happens in a simple function machine and how to link an addition fact to its complementary subtraction fact, for example working out what entered a machine when we know what left.
- Pupils should be able to look at a known number fact and work out related facts, for example if 24 + 37 = 61 then 61 – 37 = 24.
- The pairs of numbers to be subtracted are close, so simple counting skills should be used.

Challenge

Encourage a wide range of number pairs, especially large numbers that have a difference of 25. Talk about checking the subtraction with an addition.

SUPPORTING ACTIVITIES

- See further activities in *Numeracy Activity Book Year 3:* addition problems pages 32–41, subtraction facts pages 52–61.
- Pupils have demonstration teaching clocks. Tell them to show a time such as 3.45 then show the time 25 minutes later. Repeat for different times and different additions.

Vocabulary
hour, minute, a.m., p.m., morning, afternoon, evening, night, later, earlier, midnight, midday, noon
add, addition, plus, sum, total, altogether, answer, pairs, more than
subtract, subtraction, minus, take away, difference, less than, solution

Graphs

MENTAL MATHS

- Ask questions about multiplication and division facts for 2, 3, 4, 5 and 10 times tables, and multiplication facts to 5×5. Use 'show me' activities with number cards: *Show me a pair of numbers that have a product of 20.*
- Involve pupils in answering questions about doubles and halves of numbers up to 20.
- Check that pupils know the odd and even numbers up to 100.
- Involve pupils in making up a 3-digit multiple of 10 up to the next highest multiple of 100, such as making up 730 to 800.

TEACH AND DISCUSS

Reading information from diagrams and graphs

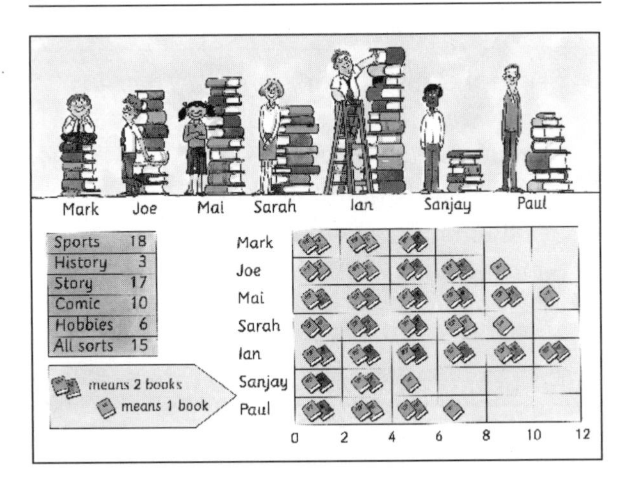

Pupil's Book: page 30

- Explain how the pictures, table and pictogram all show the same information in different ways.
- Talk about how the scale is shown on the graph and what half a picture means.
- Explain about the axes of a graph and why the numbers are on the lines, not in the spaces.
- Discuss the category 'All sorts' as shown on the table. Focus on the fact that sometimes not everything falls into nice tidy sets and so we may need an 'All sorts' set.
- Ask questions based on the three types of data-handling representation shown on the page: *Who reads most books? How many story books were read? Can we tell who read story books?*

Pupil's Book: page 31

- Talk about the pictogram shown on the page. Decide whether responses are to be verbal or recorded.
- Discuss how to collect the information about favourite colours.

Challenge

Discuss how to collect the information about hair colour and eye colour. Query whether one or two graphs will be needed.

SUPPORTING ACTIVITIES

- Involve pupils in reading and interpreting information from various sources in the classroom and from magazines.
- Discuss voting for favourite things and issues such as tallies to make a frequency table. Query what happens if someone does not have a favourite.

Vocabulary
count, tally, sort, vote, group, set, represent
graph, pictogram, table, chart, list, symbol, sign, label, information, data, axes, axis, title
most popular, least popular, most common, least common

Review

MENTAL MATHS

- Question quick recall of addition and subtraction facts of numbers within 20. Include the relationship between the two operations – how an addition is the opposite of subtraction.
- Ask questions about multiplication and division facts for 2, 3, 4, 5 and 10 times tables, and multiplication facts to 5 × 5. Use 'show me' activities with number cards: *Show me a pair of numbers that have a product of 24.*
- Discuss how addition, subtraction, multiplication and division are all linked, for example how subtraction undoes addition, how multiplication is repeated addition, how division undoes multiplication, how division is repeated subtraction, and so on.

Pupil's Book: pages 32 and 33

The pupil pages give the opportunity to assess and review:

- odd and even numbers
- multiplication and division facts for 2, 3, 4, 5, 10 times tables
- doubling and halving
- simple fractions of shapes and quantities
- relationships between addition and subtraction
- telling the time and simple time calculations.

Other areas for discussion should include:

Use counting-on skills

Check pupils can:

- count on and back by a small number to a range of numbers
- find close differences
- count in tens and hundreds from various numbers.

Knowing about 20

Check pupils know number facts for numbers up to 20 and can halve and double numbers up to 20.

Complements

Check pupils can find complements of numbers to make the next multiple of 10.

Key vocabulary
Counting and place value *hundreds, relationship, one hundred more, one hundred less, approximate, approximately, hundreds boundary*
Fractions *whole, half, quarter, third, tenth, two-thirds, three-quarters*
Adding and subtracting *add, subtract, plus, minus, total, equals, operation, sign, calculate*
Handling data *graph, diagram, chart, pictogram, axis, axes*
Strategies *count on, count back, near double, round up, check*

Use pupil pages 34 and 35 to talk about some activities which have been covered in the previous term's work.

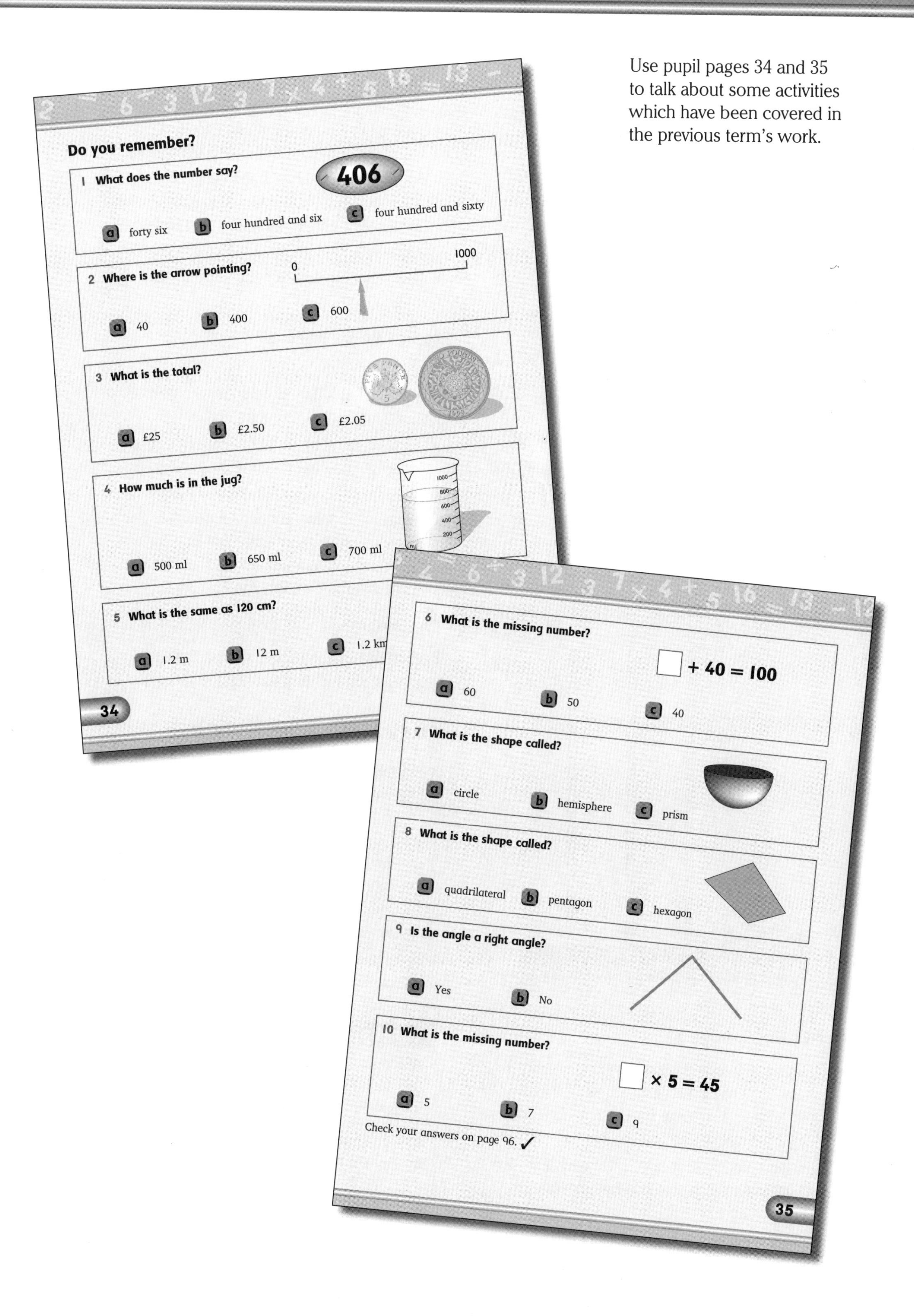

Do you remember?

1 **What does the number say?** 406

a forty six   b four hundred and six   c four hundred and sixty

2 **Where is the arrow pointing?** 0 … 1000

a 40   b 400   c 600

3 **What is the total?**

a £25   b £2.50   c £2.05

4 **How much is in the jug?**

a 500 ml   b 650 ml   c 700 ml

5 **What is the same as 120 cm?**

a 1.2 m   b 12 m   c 1.2 km

34

6 **What is the missing number?** $\square + 40 = 100$

a 60   b 50   c 40

7 **What is the shape called?**

a circle   b hemisphere   c prism

8 **What is the shape called?**

a quadrilateral   b pentagon   c hexagon

9 **Is the angle a right angle?**

a Yes   b No

10 **What is the missing number?** $\square \times 5 = 45$

a 5   b 7   c 9

Check your answers on page 96. ✓

35

Place value

MENTAL MATHS

- Involve pupils in counting forwards and back in tens and hundreds from zero. This should be done in unison to a rhythm such as a clapping pattern. Extend to counting and back from numbers other than zero.
- Question quick recall of addition and subtraction facts of numbers within 20. Include the relationship between the two operations – how an addition is the opposite of subtraction.
- Talk about multiples of 100 that total 1000, for example 600 and 400.
- Check that pupils can mentally add 2-digit multiples of 10 which cross 100, such as 70 + 50.

TEACH AND DISCUSS

Place value, ordering and estimating numbers

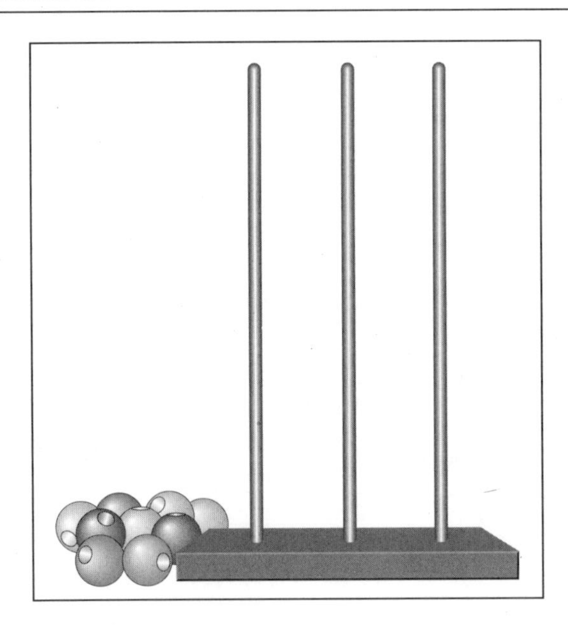

Pupil's Book: page 36

- Tell pupils to place counters on the spike abacus to create 321. Explain how this is 300 + 20 + 1. Repeat for other 2-digit and 3-digit numbers.
- Discuss making numbers 100 more/less. Ask what has to happen and whether 100 counters are needed.
- Ask pupils to use 4 counters to make a multiple of 10. Discuss alternatives and why no counters will be on the ones spike. Similarly ask them to make multiples of 100.
- Ask them to use 4 counters to make numbers that are: between 300 and 100; more than 300; less than 100.
- Talk about the number of counters needed on the ones spike to make even/odd numbers.
- Tell pupils to answer the problems on the page.

Pupil's Book: page 37

- Talk about the number line at the top of the page. Check that pupils know the value of the 'missing' numbers.
- Explain how to round numbers to the nearest 10 using the number line to help.
- Explain how we often have to work out the value of division marks on number lines and measuring instruments. We also have to approximate a value when the marker is not exactly on a division mark.

Challenge

Encourage a systematic approach to the investigation rather than random trial and error.

SUPPORTING ACTIVITIES

- Pupils work in co-operating groups. Each member records a different 2-digit number on a piece of card. Ask the group: *Who has the largest/smallest number? Who has a number that comes after 50? Who has a number that comes before 25? Who has a number that ends in 5? Place all your numbers in order.*
- See further activities in *Numeracy Activity Book Year 3* pages 12–22.

Vocabulary
place value, digits, tens, hundreds, ones/units, value, worth, 1-digit, 2-digit, 3-digit, stands for, represents
hundred more, hundred less, between, next to, compare, order
round, approximately, about, nearly, just over, just under, close to, nearest, half-way

Addition

MENTAL MATHS

- Talk about doubling and halving whole numbers up to 20. Extend to questioning about near doubles and quick methods of totalling these.
- Question quick recall of addition and subtraction facts of numbers within 20. Include the relationship between the two operations – how an addition is the opposite of subtraction.
- Talk about numbers to 100. Include: odd and even numbers within 100; pairs of numbers that make 100; rounding up to 100.
- Involve pupils in finding doubles of multiples of 5 to 50, for example double 35.

TEACH AND DISCUSS

Addition facts

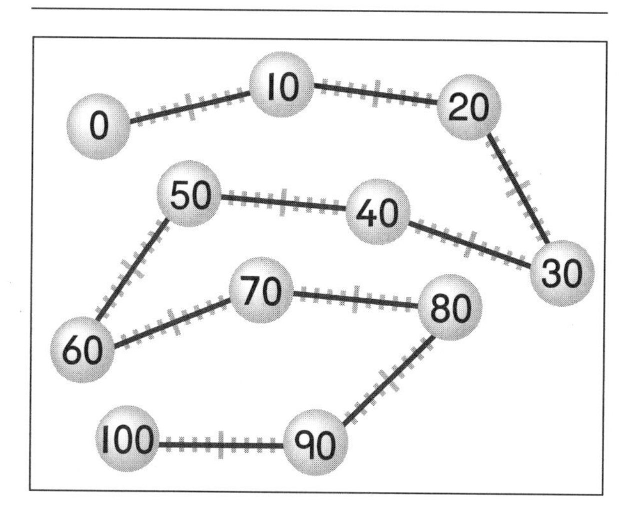

Pupil's Book: page 38

Pupils need a marker or counter that can point to individual numbers on the number line.

- Talk about the number line on the pupil page. Query whether it can be used even though some numbers are missing. Make note of the 'fives' position and how this can be used.
- Tell pupils to show where 34 is on the line. Ask for the counter to be moved to show 10, 20, 30 more. Ask whether it is necessary to count along the line in ones.
- Involve pupils in adding a single digit to nominated numbers. Query if the line can be used to help.
- Ask pupils to find the difference between two close numbers, questioning whether counting on from smaller to larger or counting back from larger to smaller makes a difference.

Pupil's Book: page 39

- Talk about good strategies to use when adding up sets of three or four small numbers. This could include looking for pairs that total 10 or 20 and knowing quick methods of adding on 9.
- Talk about strategies for adding together pairs of 2-digit numbers. Question how the number line might be helpful for some additions.

Challenge

The challenge asks for additions that go beyond the scope of the number line. Finding differences between numbers that are not close is also asked for.

SUPPORTING ACTIVITIES

- See further activities in *Numeracy Activity Book Year 3:* addition facts using small numbers pages 22–31, addition of 2-digit numbers pages 32–41.

Vocabulary
add, more, plus, make, sum, total, altogether, double, near double, how many more?, count on, equals, sign, equation
make ten, make a hundred, tens boundary, hundreds boundary
method, how?, another way, explain, tell me, show me, calculate, mentally calculate

Addition and subtraction

MENTAL MATHS

- Ask questions about multiplication and division facts for 2, 3, 4, 5 and 10 times tables, and multiplication facts to 5 × 5. Use 'show me' activities with number cards: Show me a multiple of 2 and 3.
- Involve pupils in counting forwards and back in twos from different starting numbers. This should be done to a regular rhythm such as clapping patterns or swinging weight.
- Talk about numbers to 100. Include: odd and even numbers within 100; pairs of numbers that make 100; rounding up to 100.
- Check that pupils can mentally add 2-digit numbers to multiples of 10, crossing 100, such as 76 + 50. Use simple 'show me' apparatus such as place value arrow cards, number generators, digit flips.

TEACH AND DISCUSS

Understanding addition and subtraction

Pupil's Book: page 40

Pupils use digit cards to cover up the grid to create different sums. Decide whether one set of digit cards is to be used or two sets. This affects the range of answers. Pupils can work in co-operating groups, each pupil contributing to the activity.

- *Choose the digits 2, 4, 7 and 8. Which answers can you make?*
- Choose a total such as 56 and challenge pupils to make different sums to match that answer.
- Randomly choose a digit. Tell pupils to place that digit on their grid but once placed the digit cannot be moved. Explain that they are trying to create a sum whose total is as near to 50 as possible. Repeat for three more randomly chosen digits. Discuss the answers that have been created.
- Pupils answer the problems shown on the page, writing down their results.

Pupil's Book: page 41

- For the missing signs activity it is often helpful to have them written on small pieces of paper to be arranged on the page.
- Discuss strategies for rounding up numbers to 100. Talk about rounding to the next tens number then the jump to 100. Unmarked number lines are helpful.
- Talk about checking the addition or subtraction with an equivalent calculation.
- Decide whether the answers to the various sums should be verbal or recorded.

Challenge

Pupils should write numbers on small pieces of paper and then arrange them on the triangle. Check that pupils realise they must choose their own side total and that there is no limit.

SUPPORTING ACTIVITIES

- See further activities in *Numeracy Activity Book Year 3:* addition facts using small numbers pages 22–31, addition of 2-digit numbers pages 32–41, subtraction facts with small numbers pages 42–51, subtraction of 2-digit numbers pages 52–61.

Vocabulary
add, more, plus, make, sum, total, altogether, double, near double, how many more?, count on, equals, sign
subtract, take away, minus, difference, leave, how many fewer?, how many less?, count back
method, how?, another way, explain, tell me, show me, calculate, mentally calculate

Money and problems

MENTAL MATHS

- Question quick recall of addition and subtraction facts of numbers within 20. Include the relationship between the two operations – how an addition is the opposite of subtraction.
- Involve pupils in finding doubles of multiples of 5 to 50, for example double 35.
- Pupils work in small co-operating groups, each making a different 3-digit number. Ask questions of the groups, for example: *Who has a multiple of 5? Who has the largest/smallest number? Who has an even/odd number? Who has the number nearest to 500? Arrange your numbers in order.*
- Ask pupils to halve multiples of 10 to 100. Responses can be volunteer answers or part of 'show me' activities.

TEACH AND DISCUSS

Equivalences and calculations with money

Pupil's Book: page 42

Use the pupil page to talk about the prices of the fruit and vegetables.

- Discuss items bought by weight and those bought as individual items.
- Ask why it may not be possible to buy exactly a kilogram of apples.
- Check that pupils know how to work out the change.
- Ensure that pupils know how to make up a simple bill and total it.
- Decide whether a calculator should be part of the activity.
- Tell pupils to answer the problems on the page, recording their answers as a 'sum'.

Pupil's Book: page 43

Some pupils will find it helpful to 'model' the word problems using counters and coins. They should act out each stage of the problem.

Challenge

Check that pupils know that they should choose three from the parcels shown to create different totals less than £5.

SUPPORTING ACTIVITIES

- See further activities in *Numeracy Activity Book Year 3* pages 25, 27, 31, 37, 47 and 51.
- Practical problems using catalogues, holiday brochures, etc., working within budgets, calculating change and totalling.

Vocabulary
coins, total, change, pence, pound, price, cost, cheap, dear, expensive, altogether, amount, buy, spend, how much?
count on, count back, add together, take away, how much more?
exchange, swap, worth the same, worth more, worth less

Shape and space

MENTAL MATHS

- Ask questions about multiplication and division tables for 2, 3, 4, 5, 10, and multiplication facts to 5 × 5.
- Involve pupils in using counting skills to answer mental calculations with 'large numbers'. Include: finding close differences for numbers such as 233 and 236; adding and subtracting a small number and a large number such as 345 + 4 and 568 – 5; adding and subtracting 10 and 100 with a range of numbers. Decide whether to include bridging activities such as finding the difference between 158 and 161.
- Explain how to make up a number to the next multiple of 10 or 100, for example: *What must be added to 124 to make 130? What must be added to 450 to make 500?*
- Check that pupils can mentally add or subtract a multiple of 10 to and from 2-digit numbers across the 100 boundary, for example 112 – 30 and 87 + 70.

TEACH AND DISCUSS
Positions and symmetry

Pupil's Book: page 44

- Pupils use the illustrations to make the various Multilink models.
- Groups of pupils should then pool their ideas and suggest different ways of sorting the models. *What if the models have to be put into two sets, three sets, four sets, ...?*
- Discuss what makes a model symmetrical. Decide whether the colour is an important attribute in the symmetry.
- Pupils should work in co-operating groups on the bottom three problems.

Pupil's Book: page 45

- As well as copying the given example to make symmetrical shapes, pupils should be encouraged to create their own. Talk about the line of symmetry.
- Check that pupils remember the names of the compass points.
- When describing the journey, decide whether responses should be verbal or recorded.

Challenge

The symmetrical letters can be upper and lower case. The symmetrical words could be grouped into those having the line of symmetry of each letter in the same direction, and those that don't.

SUPPORTING ACTIVITIES

- Making symmetrical patterns and shapes on pegboards and geoboards.
- Making symmetrical patterns with non-cube interlocking shapes such as Multilink Isos and prisms, Clixi, Polydron, Lego.
- Using a magnetic compass to plan a journey around school.
- Using the language of turning and movement in PE lessons.

Vocabulary
patterns, symmetrical pattern, repeating pattern, reflection, repeat, match, half, line of symmetry
position, N S E W, compass direction, underneath, centre, over, under, opposite, between, next to, diagonally, turn, half turn, clockwise, anticlockwise
circle, triangle, square, rectangle, semi-circle, pentagon, hexagon, octagon, quadrilateral, oval, rhombus, diamond

Time and weight

MENTAL MATHS

- Question quick recall of addition and subtraction facts of numbers within 20. Include the relationship between the two operations – how an addition is the opposite of subtraction.
- Involve pupils in counting forwards and back in twos, fives and tens from different starting numbers. This should be done to a regular rhythm such as clapping patterns or swinging weight.
- Talk about multiples of 100 that total 1000, for example 700 and 300.
- Check that pupils can mentally add or subtract a multiple of 10 to and from 2-digit numbers across the 100 boundary, for example 115 – 40 and 63 + 80.

TEACH AND DISCUSS

Telling the time and weighing

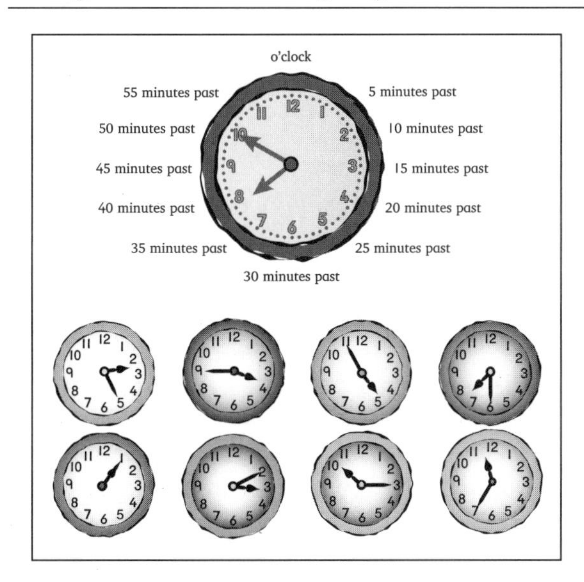

Pupil's Book: page 46

- Talk about telling the time using the illustrations on the pupil page.
- Talk about one hour later: *Show me the clock that shows one hour after 2.45.*
- Discuss morning o'clock times and afternoon o'clock times: *What are we doing at 1 o'clock in the morning? What are we doing at 1 o'clock in the afternoon?* Refer to a.m. and p.m.
- Talk about 12 noon and 12 midnight.

Pupil's Book: page 47

- Talk about the equivalence between grams, kilograms and half kilograms. Check that pupils can record in mixed units such as 1 kg and 500 g.
- Look at the scales and talk about what the divisions represent. Refer to nearest half kilogram reading.

Challenge

- Decide on how the bags are to be manufactured and what is a sensible size given that weights are to be placed inside.
- Discuss what will make the experiment a fair one.
- Pupils should decide how they are going to show their findings.

SUPPORTING ACTIVITIES

- Use a real battery clock from which the minute hand has been removed. Show how the time can be approximated just using the hour hand: *It is nearly 2 o'clock. It has just passed 10 o'clock. It is half-way between 10 and 11 o'clock.*
- Talk about time events with pupils, using vocabulary such as *old, new, takes a long time, takes a short time, how often, rarely, never, always, usually, once, twice, sometimes, takes longer, takes less time, …*
- Involve pupils in practical weighing activities for focusing upon approximating skills and using language such as *about half a kilogram, nearly 100 grams, just over 200 grams.*

Vocabulary
morning, afternoon, evening, a.m., p.m., night, midnight, midday, noon, hour, minute, o'clock, half past, clock, watch, hands, later, sooner
weigh, weighs, weight, balances, kilogram, gram, half kilogram, scales, heavier, lighter, heaviest, lightest
estimate, guess, nearly, just about, just over, just under, exact, close to, roughly, about the same

Review

MENTAL MATHS

- Ask questions about multiplication and division tables for 2, 3, 4, 5, 10, and multiplication facts to 5×5.
- Talk about doubling and halving whole numbers within 100. Extend to questioning about near doubles and quick methods of totalling these.
- Check that pupils can mentally add or subtract a multiple of 10 to and from 2-digit numbers across the 100 boundary, for example $115 - 40$ and $63 + 80$.
- Explain how to make up a number to the next multiple of 10 or 100, for example: *What must be added to 124 to make 130? What must be added to 450 to make 500?*

Pupil's Book: pages 48 and 49

The pupil pages give the opportunity to assess and review:

- rounding to the nearest 10
- addition skills
- simple money calculations
- names of 2-D and 3-D shapes
- telling the time at 5-minute intervals
- measuring lengths to the nearest centimetre.

Other areas for discussion should include:

Use place value ideas

Reading, writing and ordering 3-digit numbers.

Use counting on and back skills

Check pupils can:

- count on by a small number to a range of numbers
- find close differences
- count in twos, fives and tens.

Vocabulary connected to measuring weight

Check pupils understand words connected to estimating and measuring weights.

Shapes and patterns

Check pupils can talk about turning and direction, including right angles. They should also be able to recognise shapes that have lines of symmetry.

Key vocabulary
Number *hundreds, relationship, one hundred more, one hundred less, approximate, approximately*
Measuring *kilogram, gram, half kilogram, division, measuring scale*
Calculations *hundreds boundary, product, equation*
Shape *right angles, vertex, vertices, diagram, hemisphere, prism, semicircle, pentagonal, hexagonal, octagonal, quadrilateral*
Position and direction *row, column, compass point, N S E W, horizontal, vertical, diagonal, angle*
Money *note, expensive, amount, value*

Numbers and counting patterns

MENTAL MATHS

- Count on or back in tens and hundreds from any 2- or 3-digit number in unison to clapping rhythms.
- Recall of addition and subtraction for each number up to 20 as 'show me' with digit cards.
- State subtraction fact corresponding to addition fact and vice versa, using trios such as 5, 7 and 12.
- Ask questions about mentally adding and subtracting a single digit to and from a 2-digit number bridging a tens number, for example 67 + 7.

TEACH AND DISCUSS

Numbers and number sequences

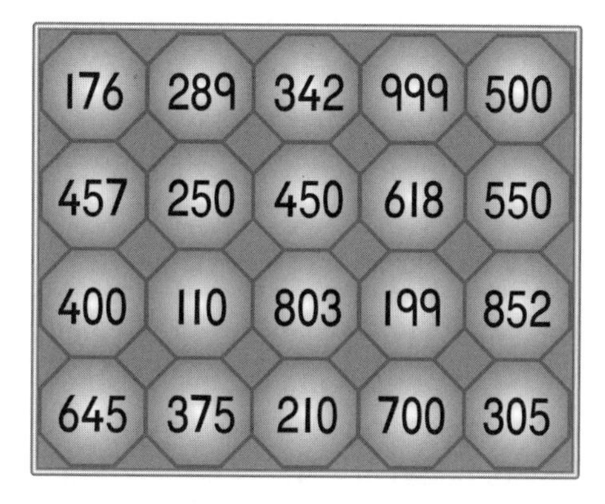

Pupil's Book: page 50

Each pupil will need counters to cover some of the numbers on their grid.

Number recognition

- *Cover up this number: 250, 700, 199, …*
- Check that pupils can recognise and say 3-digit numbers.

Odd and even numbers

- *Cover up an odd number.* Discuss alternatives, and that end digits of odd numbers will be 1, 3, 5, 7 or 9.
- *Cover up an even number.* Discuss alternatives and that end digits of even numbers will be 0, 2, 4, 6 or 8. Check that pupils realise that zero is not an even number.

Comparing numbers

- *Cover up a number that is more than 400.* Discuss alternatives.
- *Cover up a number that is less than 200.* Discuss alternatives.

Pupils should complete the problems on the pupil page.

Pupil's Book: page 51

- Involve pupils in counting on in steps of 3, 4 or 5 from any small number to at least 50 and back again.
- Discuss the number sequences on the page and what is needed to make each one a pattern.
- Check that pupils know that number sequences can ascend and descend.

Challenge

Pupils should work in co-operating groups on the investigation.

SUPPORTING ACTIVITIES

- Write 250< □ on the board. Ask for volunteers to come and record possible solutions. Similarly write 300 > □ and ask for solutions.
- Write 150 □ 200 on the board. Ask for possible numbers that come between these numbers.
- Decide whether to challenge pupils with 150 < □ < 200.
- Ask pupils to count on by a small number to 2- and 3-digit numbers.
- See further activities in *Numeracy Activity Book Year 3* pages 6–9 and 14–17.

Vocabulary
odd, even, digit, tens, hundreds, ones, sequence, count on, count back, more than, less than, greater than, multiples, order, size
start from, start with, start at, look at, put, place, carry on, continue, describe, decide, talk about, explain, record, complete
same, different, missing numbers, number grid, number square, counters

Addition and problems

MENTAL MATHS

- Ask questions about finding doubles and near doubles of numbers in the 0 to 100 range, especially of multiples of 5.
- Ask questions about halving numbers. Include halving all numbers within 1 to 20 and multiples of 10.
- Play 'tell me about'. Choose numbers and shapes as the target of the discussion. Encourage lots of different facts about the same target. Record on the board as appropriate.
- Check that pupils can mentally work out close differences of numbers which are either side of a multiple of 100, for example 398 and 402.

TEACH AND DISCUSS

Totalling 2-digit numbers

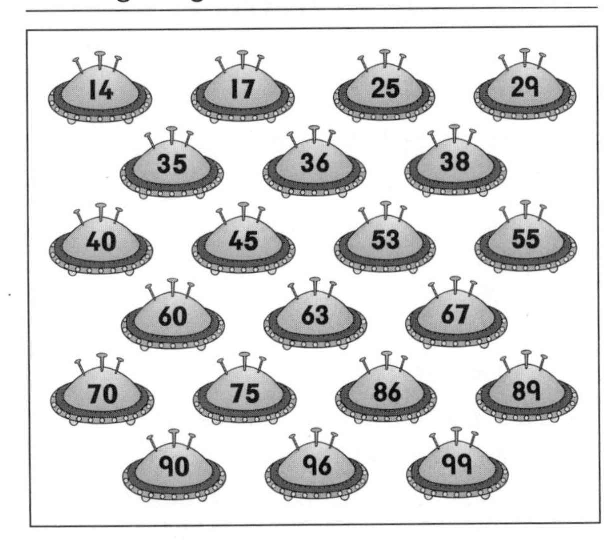

Pupil's Book: page 52

Pupils place counters on the page to indicate their responses to activities such as these.

- *Cover up the largest/smallest number.*
- *Cover numbers that are more than 50.*
- *Cover numbers that are less than 68.*
- *Cover numbers that are between 50 and 80.*
- *Cover up a number that is an eighty and a six.*

Let pupils work in co-operating groups where each pupil chooses a different number to cover. Ask questions of the group, who decide which member should respond. For example:

- *Who in the group has the largest/smallest number?*
- *Who in the group has the number nearest to 75?*

Pupils should answer the problems on the page, writing down their results.

Explain strategies such as breaking into tens and ones and recombining, and informal pencil and paper methods such as unmarked number lines.

Pupil's Book: page 53

- Discuss the strategies that can or should be used to calculate the sums on the page.
- Talk about the strategies of partitioning into tens and ones and recombining.

Challenge

Pupils should decide how to record their results. Encourage a systematic approach rather than random selections. Pupils can work independently on this activity.

SUPPORTING ACTIVITIES

- See further activities in *Numeracy Activity Book Year 3:* addition facts using small numbers pages 22–31, addition of 2-digit numbers pages 32–41.
- Draw a large triangle on the board and write 100 in the centre. Explain that numbers at the corners must total the number in the middle. Pupils explore some solutions. Include rules such as: all the numbers must be 2-digit numbers; all the numbers must be even numbers; all the numbers must be multiples of 5.

Vocabulary
add, more, plus, make, sum, total, altogether, double, near double, how many more?, count on, equals, sign
make ten, make a hundred, tens boundary, hundreds boundary
method, how?, another way, explain, tell me, show me, calculate, mentally calculate

Division

MENTAL MATHS

- Ask questions about multiplication and division facts, encouraging quick recall for 2, 5 and 10 times tables. Pupils should be able to quickly recall some of the 3 times table facts.
- Extend multiplying and dividing by 10 to facts beyond the 10 times table.
- Ask questions about finding doubles and near doubles of numbers in the 0 to 100 range, especially of multiples of 5.
- Ask questions about halving numbers. Include halving all numbers within 1 to 20 and multiples of 10.

TEACH AND DISCUSS

Learning division facts

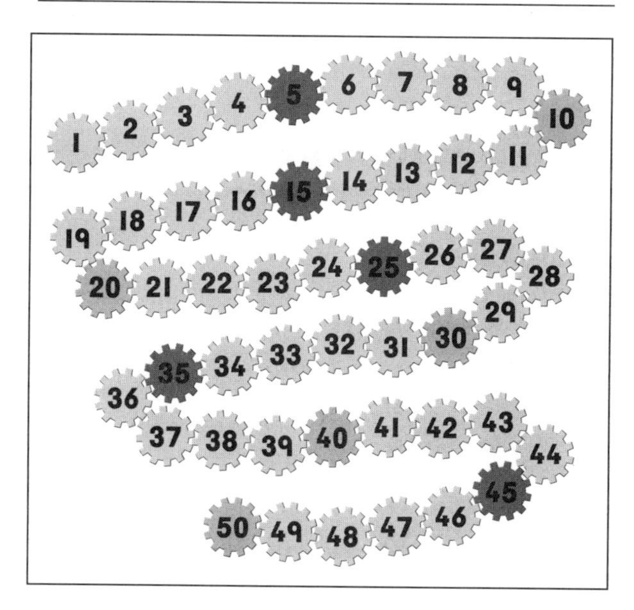

Pupil's Book: page 54

Pupils hop along the line with a marker, making jumps of 2, 3, 4 etc. Check that pupils make complete jumps rather than in ones.

Ask questions such as these:

- *Start on zero and make jumps of 2. Which numbers do we land on?*
- *What if we start on 50 and jump back in twos?*
- *Start on zero. How many jumps of 2 will reach 12?*
- *Start on zero. Where will five jumps of 2 take us?*

The questions on the pupil page can be answered verbally or be recorded.

Pupil's Book: page 55

- Talk about the division sign and what it means.
- Explain that pupils can use the number line to help work out the answers.
- Talk about multiplication undoing division, and vice versa.

Challenge

Encourage pupils to investigate several different solutions for each of the open 'sums'.

SUPPORTING ACTIVITIES

- See further activities in *Numeracy Activity Book Year 3* pages 72–81.
- Involve pupils in practical activities that involve grouping and sharing, focusing on the different and complementary vocabulary for each.

Vocabulary
lots of, groups of, halve, share, share equally, divide, divided by
calculate, work out, answer, result
how many?, what is?, check, explain, show how you …, record

Fractions

MENTAL MATHS

- Ask questions about multiplication and division facts, encouraging quick recall for 2, 5 and 10 times tables. Pupils should be able to quickly recall some of the 3 times table facts.
- Extend multiplying and dividing by 10 to facts beyond the 10 times table.
- Involve pupils in dividing 3-digit multiples of 100 by 10 and 100.
- Ask questions about halving numbers. Include halving all numbers within 1 to 20 and multiples of 10.

TEACH AND DISCUSS

Finding fractions of shapes and quantities

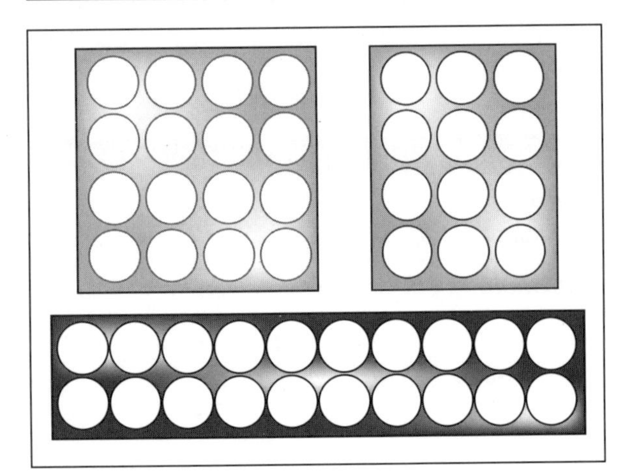

Pupil's Book: page 56

Tell pupils to cover the arrays with counters to match activities such as these:

- *Cover a half of each array. How many in each array? How many is a half?*
- *Can you cover a quarter of each array? How many in each quarter?*
- *Can you cover a tenth of each array? Which array can you show a tenth of?*
- *How many in a quarter of the first array? Show me three-quarters.*

Ask pupils to use two colours on each array. Question what fraction each colour could be.

The questions on the pupil page can be answered verbally or be written.

Pupil's Book: page 57

- Talk about estimating fractions. Involve pupils in simple comparisons such as: *Is it more than a half?*
- Talk about which fractions add up to a whole one.
- Check that pupils know some equivalent fractions to a half.

Challenge

Encourage pupils to find several solutions that satisfy the 'quarter red', 'three-quarters white' criterion.

SUPPORTING ACTIVITIES

- See further activities in *Numeracy Activity Book Year 3* pages 82–87.
- Each pupil needs a strip of card on which is threaded an elastic band. Ask pupils to slide the band to show a half, a quarter, three-quarters, a third. Use different lengths of card which can be swapped around.

Vocabulary
part, equal parts, fraction, whole one, half, halve, quarter, three-quarters, third, two-thirds, tenth
divide into, share, share equally
estimate, guess, nearly, just about, just over, just under, exact, close to, roughly, about the same

Bar charts

MENTAL MATHS

- Ask questions about multiplication and division facts, encouraging quick recall for 2, 5 and 10 times tables. Pupils should be able to quickly recall some of the 3 times table facts.
- Play 'tell me about'. Choose numbers and shapes as the target of the discussion. Encourage lots of different facts about the same target. Record on the board as appropriate.
- Check that pupils can mentally work out close differences of numbers which are either side of a multiple of 100, for example 398 and 402.
- State a subtraction fact corresponding to an addition fact and vice versa, using trios such as 7, 6 and 13.

TEACH AND DISCUSS

Reading bar charts

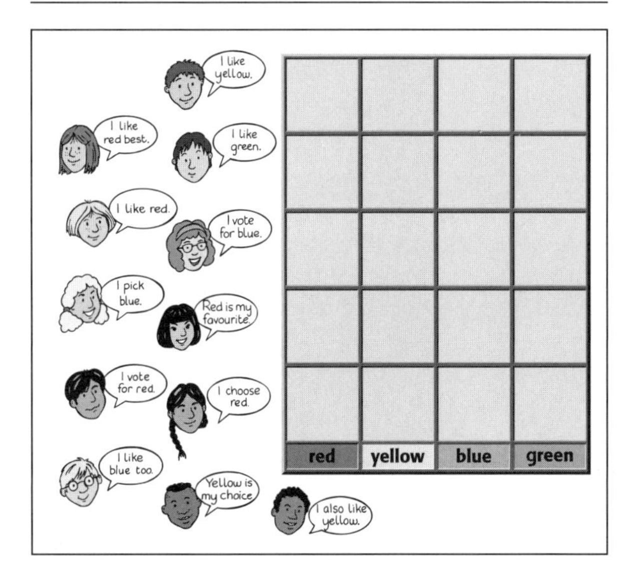

Pupil's Book: page 58

- Talk about the illustration and tell pupils to build up a graph on the page using coloured counters.
- Explain about the horizontal and vertical axes.
- Ask what information can be derived from the page.
- Decide whether the pupil questions are to be answered verbally or to be recorded.

Pupil's Book: page 59

- Talk about the graphs on the page. Check that pupils understand reading half squares.
- Refer to horizontal and vertical axes and what they show.
- Decide whether the questions are to be answered verbally or to be written.

Challenge

Discuss how the information is to be collected and how it is to be presented. Query whether the collected information would be better sorted before it is presented.

SUPPORTING ACTIVITIES

- Look for ways in which information is displayed in the classroom.
- Use commercial sources for interpreting information in various forms, such as price lists, supermarket special offers, holiday booklets.

Vocabulary
count, tally, sort, vote, group, set, represent
table, chart, list, symbol, sign, label, information, data, axis, axes, horizontal, vertical, graph, pictogram, diagram
most popular, least popular, most frequent, least frequent, most common, least common, favourite

Review

MENTAL MATHS

- Ask questions about multiplication and division facts, encouraging quick recall for 2, 5 and 10 times tables. Pupils should be able to quickly recall some of the 3 times and 4 times table facts.
- Play 'tell me about'. Choose numbers and shapes as the target of the discussion. Encourage lots of different facts about the same target. Record on the board as appropriate.
- Check that pupils can mentally add a small number to any 2-digit numbers.
- State subtraction facts corresponding to addition facts and vice versa, using trios such as 16, 9, 7.

Pupil's Book: pages 60 and 61

The pupil pages give the opportunity to assess and review:

- rounding numbers to the nearest 10
- totalling numbers
- totalling coins and giving change
- recognising right angles
- complements to 100
- measuring lines to the nearest half centimetre
- multiplication and division facts for 2, 5 and 10
- recognising simple fractions
- reading scales.

Other areas for discussion should include:

Use counting on/back skills

Check pupils can count on and back:

- by a small number from a range of numbers
- to find close differences
- in tens and hundreds
- in twos, threes, fours, fives.

Key vocabulary
Number *hundreds, relationship, one hundred more, one hundred less, approximate, approximately*
Calculations *hundreds boundary, product, equation*
Money *note, expensive, amount, value*
Fractions *one third, two-thirds, one tenth*

Use pupil pages 62 and 63 to talk about some activities which have been covered in the previous term's work.

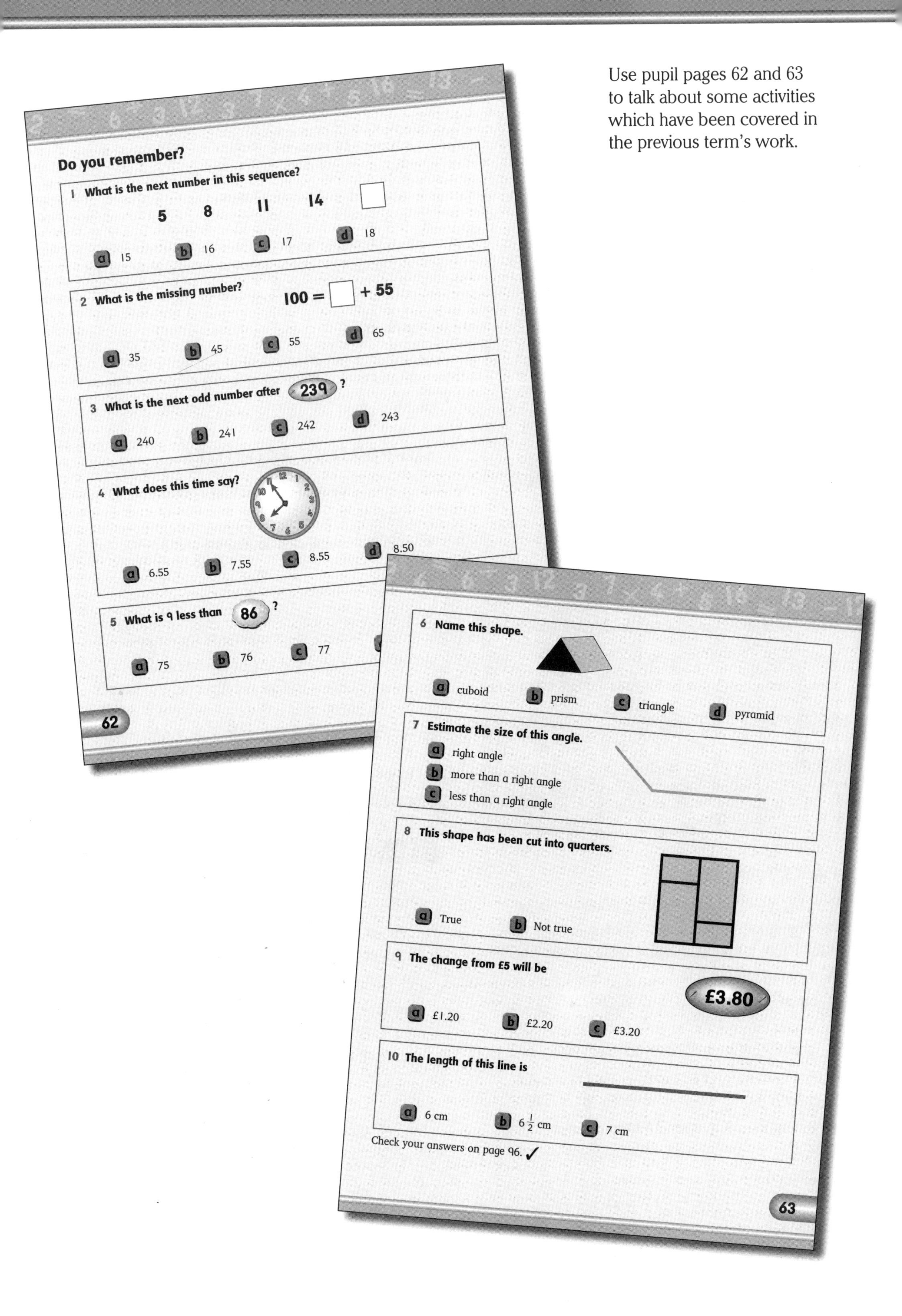

Do you remember?

1 **What is the next number in this sequence?**

5 8 11 14 ☐

a 15 b 16 c 17 d 18

2 **What is the missing number?** 100 = ☐ + 55

a 35 b 45 c 55 d 65

3 **What is the next odd number after 239?**

a 240 b 241 c 242 d 243

4 **What does this time say?**

a 6.55 b 7.55 c 8.55 d 8.50

5 **What is 9 less than 86?**

a 75 b 76 c 77

62

6 **Name this shape.**

a cuboid b prism c triangle d pyramid

7 **Estimate the size of this angle.**

a right angle
b more than a right angle
c less than a right angle

8 **This shape has been cut into quarters.**

a True b Not true

9 **The change from £5 will be** £3.80

a £1.20 b £2.20 c £3.20

10 **The length of this line is**

a 6 cm b $6\frac{1}{2}$ cm c 7 cm

Check your answers on page 96. ✓

63

Place value

MENTAL MATHS

- Pupils count on from a range of numbers in tens and hundreds. Play 'Mexican wave' where pupils in turn add on 10 whilst quickly standing up then sitting down.
- Ask pupils to make up appropriate numbers to 10, 100 and 1000. Answers can be shown on simple apparatus such as number generators, digit flips, fan numbers, place value arrow cards.
- Play 'show me' activities with number cards. Ask pupils open and closed questions about number facts to about 20. Include word problems, multi-stage problems and problems that show addition and subtraction to be reverses.

TEACH AND DISCUSS

Place value and rounding numbers

1000	2000	3000	4000	5000	6000	7000	8000	9000
100	200	300	400	500	600	700	800	900
10	20	30	40	50	60	70	80	90
1	2	3	4	5	6	7	8	9

Pupil's Book: page 64

Explain how to place counters on the place value grid to make up any whole number to at least 1000, for example placing counters on 300, 40 and 8 to make 348.

- *Show me: 259; 773; 804; 620; …*
- *Show me a number that is between: 400 and 450; 720 and 740; 822 and 836; …*
- *Show me a 3-digit number that is: odd; a multiple of 5; even and more than 770; …*
- Discuss how to round to the nearest 100.
- *Show me the 100 number nearest to: 534; 762; 850; 952; …*

The pupil questions can be oral or written responses.

Pupil's Book: page 65

Talk about the number line and the value of the divisions.

- Pupils write the numbers shown to the nearest 100 using the number line as an aid.
- Discuss rounding money to the nearest £ and how the 'rule' is the same.
- Talk about estimating positions on a 0–1000 number line and how it is possible to be fairly accurate to multiples of 100 and 10 but that other numbers are rounded off to these.

Challenge

Check that pupils order their numbers correctly. The activity can be repeated for different sets of digits.

SUPPORTING ACTIVITIES

- See further activities in *Numeracy Activity Book Year 3* pages 6–21.
- Pupils make 2-digit numbers with place value arrow cards which show hundreds, tens and ones.
- Use plastic or wood place value apparatus to model what 2-digit numbers look like.
- Play the 'same value but different picture' game. Write a 3-digit number on the board. Pupils come and write an equivalent way of expressing it, for example $468 = 400 + 60 + 8 = 450 + 18 = 470 - 2 = \square$. Focus on ways of writing that might help when calculating.

Vocabulary
place value, digits, value, worth, relationship, ending in
number words – tens, hundreds, thousands, between, after, before, odd, even, multiple
estimate, approximate, approximately, nearly, about, more, less, round up, round down, nearest to

Adding and subtracting

MENTAL MATHS

- Ask questions about multiplication and division facts for the 2, 5 and 10 times tables. Expect quick recall responses. Extend to 3 and 4 times tables as appropriate. Include open and closed questions and those that show the relationship between × and ÷. Use 'show me' activities with digit cards and fan numbers.
- Give multiples of 5 to 50 and ask pupils to double them. Ask for the complementary halves.
- Extend to asking for doubles of multiples of 50 to 500.
- Ask pupils to mentally add and subtract pairs of 2-digit numbers – not crossing tens boundaries.

TEACH AND DISCUSS

Strategies for addition of numbers

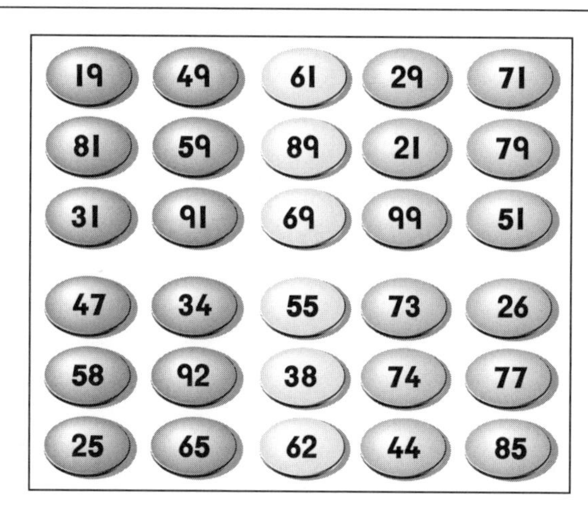

Pupil's Book: page 66

Pupils place counters on pairs of numbers, one in the top grid and another in the bottom grid.

- Discuss adding near multiples of 10 to numbers and how this can be made easier. Check that pupils understand about 'adjusting'.
- Tell them to cover nominated pairs of numbers and ask for the total, checking how it was done.
- Discuss subtracting near multiples of 10 from numbers and how this can be made easier. Check that pupils understand about 'adjusting'.
- Tell them to cover nominated pairs of numbers and ask for the difference, checking how it was done.
- Pupil questions should be done mentally. The responses can be oral or recorded.

Pupil's Book: page 67

- Before pupils work on each block of examples, ask for possible strategies that can be used to answer them.
- Some of the questions use patterns of similar calculations. Discuss these.

Challenge

Pupils should look for alternative solutions to the problem.

SUPPORTING ACTIVITIES

- Play the 'same value but different picture' game. Write a 3-digit number on the board. Pupils come and write an equivalent way of expressing it. For example 468 = 400 + 60 + 8 = 450 + 18 = 470 – 2 = ☐. Focus on ways of writing that might help when calculating.
- Play 'ping pong'. Divide the class into two lines. The first pupil in one line states a 2-digit number to which the first pupil in the opposite line adds 9. This is repeated for the subsequent pupils so that numbers 'ping pong' from one side to the other having 9 added. Similarly subtract 9.
- See further activities in *Numeracy Activity Book Year 3:* addition facts pages 32–41, subtraction facts pages 52–61.

Vocabulary
add, more, plus, make, sum, total, altogether, double, near double, how many more?, count on
subtract, take away, minus, difference, leave, how many fewer?, how many less?, count back
nearest ten, tens boundary, adjust, strategy, method, another way, investigate, round, nearly, about

Problems

MENTAL MATHS

- Ask pupils to add and subtract numbers such as 9, 19 and 29 with a range of 2-digit numbers. Check the strategy being used. Involve pupils in 'show me' activities with digit cards.
- Give multiples of 100 for pupils to make up to 1000.
- Give multiples of 5 for pupils to make up to 100.
- Ask pupils to mentally add and subtract pairs of 2-digit numbers – not crossing tens boundaries.

TEACH AND DISCUSS

Interpreting problems

Pupil's Book: page 68

- Discuss buying items in ones and in multiple packs and how a single item may contain lots of 'ones', for example *A box of biscuits contains lots of single biscuits.*
- Talk about how items are priced and why 99p is a popular price.
- Check that pupils understand decimal notation for money.
- Talk about each of the problems, asking what type of sum each requires. Query whether any can be answered in the head or whether it is easier with pencil and paper.
- Decide whether to include use of the calculator and discuss entering amounts of money into the calculator.

Pupil's Book: page 69

Pupils will be required to make up a number story for one of the blocks of activity. Check that pupils understand what this means. Encourage lots of alternatives for each example. Include a rule that the word problem must be about money.

Challenge

Encourage a systematic approach to the problem. Discuss how the results are going to be recorded.

SUPPORTING ACTIVITIES

- See further activities in *Numeracy Activity Book Year 3* pages 25, 27, 31, 37, 47 and 51.
- Practical problems using catalogues, lists, brochures, budgets, calculating totals and change. Include situations that involve the questions *Have we enough?* and *How long will it take?*

Vocabulary
coins, total, change, pence, pound, price, cost, cheap, dear, expensive, altogether, amount, buy, spend, how much?, sell, sold, buy, bought
count on, count back, add together, take away, how much more?, method, calculate, mentally calculate, how did you work it out?
exchange, swap, worth the same, worth more, worth less, value

Adding

MENTAL MATHS

- Ask pupils to add and subtract numbers such as 9, 19 and 29 with a range of 2-digit numbers. Check the strategy being used. Involve pupils in 'show me' activities with digit cards.
- Ask questions about the 3 times table, expecting fairly quick responses. Include both the multiplication and division facts.
- Involve pupils in counting on and back in threes, initially from zero but eventually from other numbers.
- Ask pupils to mentally add and subtract pairs of multiples of 100 – crossing the 1000 boundary, for example 800 + 500.

TEACH AND DISCUSS

Methods of adding 2-digit and 3-digit numbers

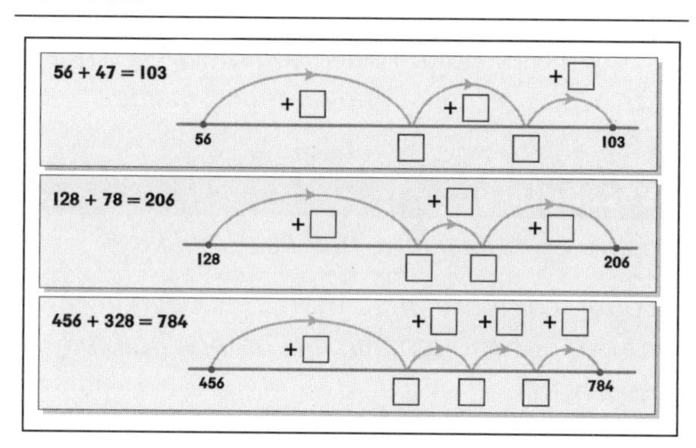

Pupil's Book: page 70

- Explain the addition number jumps on the page, focusing on the size of the jumps and the choice of these. Query the size of jump and where they land.
- Give alternative examples for pupils to solve, using an informal jumping along a blank number line strategy.

Pupil's Book: page 71

- For each block of sums discuss the strategies that should be used. Include jumping along an unmarked number track. Decide whether to include more formal recombining strategies for horizontal additions.
- Encourage discussion among pupils as to the strategies that can be used for the sums.

Challenge

Pupils should find several examples that satisfy the open problem.

SUPPORTING ACTIVITIES

- See further activities in *Numeracy Activity Book Year 3* pages 32–41.
- Write pairs of numbers on the board. Ask pupils for jumps required to move from one number to the other.

Vocabulary
add on, count back, move, hop, jump, count on to, count on by, hundreds, tens, ones
add, more, plus, make, sum, total, altogether, how many more?, count on, count back
say, read, write, record, find a different way, how?, explain, describe, answer, check

Capacity

MENTAL MATHS

- Ask pupils to add and subtract numbers such as 11, 21 and 31 with a range of 2-digit numbers. Check the strategy being used. Involve pupils in 'show me' activities with digit cards.
- Ask questions about the 3 times table, expecting fairly quick responses. Include both the multiplication and division facts.
- Give multiples of 5 to 50 and ask pupils to double them. Ask for the complementary halves. Extend to asking for doubles of multiples of 50 to 500.
- Ask pupils to mentally add and subtract pairs of multiples of 100 – crossing the 1000 boundary, for example 800 + 500.

TEACH AND DISCUSS

Litres, millilitres and approximations

Pupil's Book: page 72

- Talk about the containers shown on the page, asking how much each is likely to hold in relation to a litre. Initially accept responses such as more than a litre and less than a litre, then encourage a closer approximation.
- Discuss units of measurement that are sensible for measuring with the containers, referring to litres, half litres and millilitres. Talk about how many millilitres make a litre and half litre.
- With demonstration containers and a litre measuring jug, have pupils estimate how many millilitres in multiples of 100 ml each container holds. Discuss which estimates were 'good' estimates, reassuring pupils that estimates are rarely 'spot on'.

Pupil's Book: page 73

Check that pupils know the value of each division mark on the measuring jugs.

Challenge

Pupils estimate the 200 ml position on unusually shaped bottles, marking the level with an elastic band. This estimation must then be checked out. Pupils discuss how it can be checked.

SUPPORTING ACTIVITIES

- Involve pupils in practical and written problem-solving activities, for example *How long will a bottle of medicine last if we have to take 2 spoons 3 times a day?*
- Compare commercial packages and how much they hold: *Which containers are full to the top and which have 'room' inside?*

Vocabulary
capacity, holds, litre, half litre, millilitre
count, compare, how many?, enough, too much, not enough, fill, full, empty, half full, nearly full
estimate, guess, nearly, just about, just over, just under, exact, close to, roughly, about the same

Shape and space

MENTAL MATHS

- Involve pupils in using counting skills to answer mental calculations with 'large numbers'. Include: finding close differences for numbers such as 238 and 241; adding and subtracting a small number and a large number such as 345 + 4 and 568 – 5; adding and subtracting 10 and 100 with a range of numbers. Include bridging activities such as adding 357 and 4.
- Ask open and closed questions about the 2, 3, 5 and 10 times tables, using digit cards as part of 'show me' activities.
- Pupils should count on in tens and hundreds from a range of 2-digit and 3-digit numbers.
- Check that pupils can mentally calculate adding pairs of 2-digit numbers that cross the hundred boundary, such as 45 and 72.

TEACH AND DISCUSS

Positions and properties of shapes

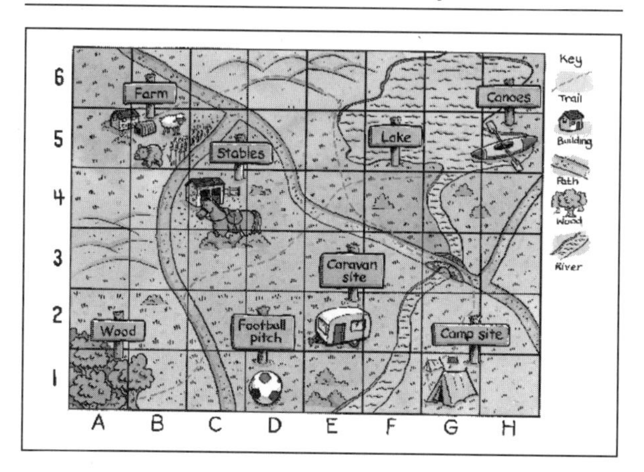

Pupil's Book: page 74

- Talk about the plan on the pupil page and what it is showing.
- Focus on the grid lines, numbers and letters, explaining why they are there and how they are used.
- Ask pupils to describe the position of nominated items on the grid.
- Pupils should move a counter around the grid, following instructions, to see where the mystery journey ends up.

Pupil's Book: page 75

- Check that pupils can recognise right angles and lines of symmetry in simple 2-D shapes.
- Discuss angles that are more than and less than a right angle. Use the corner of a folded piece of paper as a 'right angle checker'.
- Pupils should choose their own shape when drawing reflections. Use plain, squared and isometric paper.

Challenge

The words *symmetrical* and *not symmetrical* raise discussion points. Some shapes have rotational symmetry but not line symmetry – the parallelogram is one such example. Decide whether to address this or avoid until later.

SUPPORTING ACTIVITIES

- Each pupil should use hinged geostrips to make angles that are right angles, less than a right angle and more than a right angle. Include a straight line of two right angles.
- Pupils should find all the lines of symmetry of 2-D shapes which have been cut out of paper. These can be found by folding. Include shapes that have no lines of symmetry.
- Explore and test general statements about shapes, such as: *All rectangles have 4 right angles, A triangle has no more than one right angle, Squares always have 4 lines of symmetry.*

Vocabulary
symmetrical, line of symmetry, reflection, mirror line, fold, match, pattern
position, horizontal, vertical, diagonally, grid, row, column, map, plan, up, down, left, right, N S E W, journey, route
angle, right angle, more than a right angle, less than a right angle, a straight line, turn, half turn, quarter turn

Review

MENTAL MATHS

- Involve pupils in talking about shapes and numbers: *What can you tell me about this shape? What can we say about 100?*
- Ask open and closed questions about 2, 3, 5 and 10 times tables, using digit cards as part of 'show me' activities.
- Test pupils' recall for number facts to 20 through open and closed questions as part of 'show me' activities with digit cards or fan numbers.

Pupil's Book: pages 76 and 77

The pupil pages give the opportunity to assess and review:

- rounding to the nearest 100
- ordering 3-digit numbers
- totalling three or more numbers
- estimation of number positions within 1000
- totalling multiples of 100
- informal and formal addition strategies
- recognition of times and shapes.

Other areas for discussion should include:

- mental strategies for simple calculations, such as adding and subtracting 9 and multiplying by 10.

Key vocabulary
Number *hundreds, relationship*
Measuring *litre, millilitre*
Calculation *hundreds boundary, product, method, equation*
Money *note, amount, value, expensive*
Shape *right angled, quadrilateral, map, plan, grid, row, column, angle, horizontal, vertical, diagonal*

Numbers

MENTAL MATHS

- Ask pupils to round numbers to the nearest 10 or 100. They should hold up simple apparatus such as place value arrow cards, number generators and digit flips to indicate their answers.
- Pupils work in small co-operative groups, each writing down a different 3-digit number. Ask the groups questions such as: *Who has the largest/smallest number? A multiple of 5/10? An odd/even number?* Pupils should arrange their numbers in order.
- Encourage quick recall of multiplication and division facts for the 4 times table. Include revision of 2, 3, 5 and 10 times tables.
- Check that pupils can add and subtract multiples of 10 with 2-digit and 3-digit numbers, crossing the 100 boundary, for example 87 + 60 and 325 – 30.

TEACH AND DISCUSS

Recognising multiples

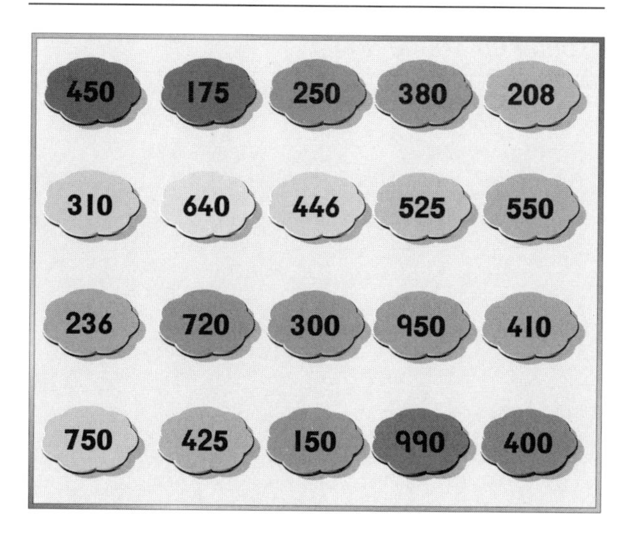

Pupil's Book: page 78

- Talk about multiples of 5, 10, 50 and 100, asking for examples of each. Include multiples of 2 and how these are the set of even numbers.
- Pupils place counters on the grid to show an example of a multiple of: 2, 5, 10, 50 and 100. Discuss the alternatives.
- Ask pupils to look for and cover pairs that total 1000.
- The answers to the questions on the page should be written down.

Pupil's Book: page 79

The missing number sequences can be completed orally or else pupils copy and complete in their books. Discuss how each pattern would continue.

Challenge

Check that pupils understand that 'next door numbers' are consecutive numbers. Check whether solutions are found by trial and error or by trial and improvement.

SUPPORTING ACTIVITIES

- Have pupils count in different multiples, forwards and back. This should be done in unison in time to a rhythm or clapping pattern.
- Involve pupils in solving a wide range of number puzzles such as magic squares and arithmogons. These are usually easier if the numbers to be used are written on small pieces of card.

Vocabulary
multiples, fives, twos, tens, fifties, hundreds, ones, threes, fours
odd, even, pair, number pattern, sequence, every other, more than, less than
count, count on, count back, count to, before, after, order, complete

Remainders

MENTAL MATHS

- Encourage quick recall of multiplication and division facts for the 4 times table. Include revision of the 2, 3, 5 and 10 times tables.
- Talk about the links between × and ÷ and how one undoes the other. Ask pupils to give a division fact based on a multiplication fact.
- Discuss using place value and number fact knowledge to work out answers such as: *If* $3 \times 4 = 12$ *what is* 3×40*?*
- Check that pupils can add and subtract multiples of 10 with 2-digit and 3-digit numbers, crossing the 100 boundary, for example 87 + 60 and 325 – 30.

TEACH AND DISCUSS

Remainders and rounding remainders

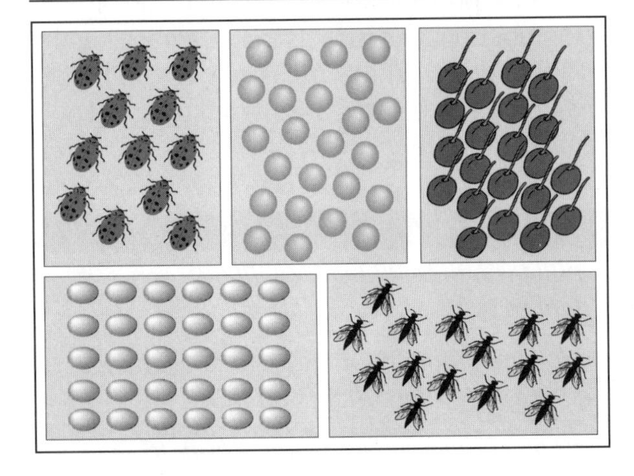

Pupil's Book: page 80

- Explain that the 'gulper' will visit each of the sets in turn. The question is, will any be left after the visit? It will help some pupils if they copy each set with counters.
- Discuss the size of remainder which is possible when dividing by 2, 3, 4 and 5.
- Check that pupils realise that sometimes there might be no remainders. Query which numbers leave no remainders, linking these numbers to the multiples of the divisor.
- Decide how pupils will respond to the questions on the page.

Pupil's Book: page 81

- Discuss with pupils which aids will help the calculations and whether any are needed at all.
- Decide how the answers are to be recorded.
- Talk about rounding up remainders and rounding down remainders.

Challenge

Check that pupils realise that they are looking for remainders. Although the activity is fairly simple, the presentation is quite sophisticated.

SUPPORTING ACTIVITIES

- See further activities in *Numeracy Activity Book Year 3* pages 72–81.
- Play 'The remainder is… What is the division?' Encourage lots of examples which match the given remainder.

Vocabulary
divide, share, remainder, equal groups, divided by, divided into, left over
sign, division, symbol, equation, equals, answer, result
exactly, not exactly, about, approximately, round up, round down

Money and problems

MENTAL MATHS

- Ask pupils for doubles of multiples of 5 to 50 and the corresponding halves.
- Test for finding doubles of multiples of 50 to 500 and the corresponding halves.
- Question quick methods of adding and subtracting near multiples of 10, such as 9 and 11. Include 2-digit and 3-digit numbers in these quick mental calculations.
- Check that pupils can mentally multiply 2-digit multiples of 10 (to 50) by 2, 3, 4, 5 and 10, for example 20×4.

TEACH AND DISCUSS

The importance of checking results when solving problems

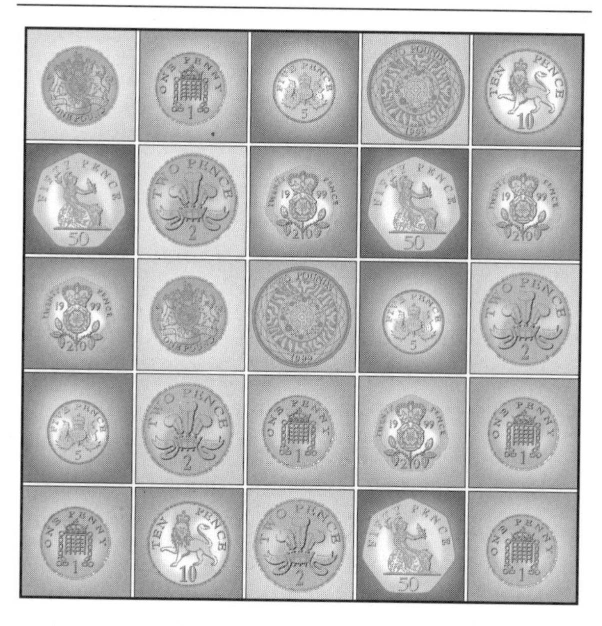

Pupil's Book: page 82

Pupils will place counters on the grid.

- *Cover three coins and tell me the total.*
- *What is the largest total you can make with three of these coins?*
- *I will tell you an amount. You cover the change from £1.*
- *Show me £1.50.* Discuss alternative solutions.
- Pupils should work in small groups to solve the problems on the page.

Pupil's Book: page 83

- Explain that the page is about numbers and signs that have gone missing. The pupils' task is to solve the missing number problems.
- For each block of activities discuss possible strategies for solving them.

Challenge

It often helps to have the operation signs written on small pieces of card. These can then be arranged on the page.

SUPPORTING ACTIVITIES

- See further activities in *Numeracy Activity Book Year 3* pages 25, 27, 31, 37, 47 and 51.
- Involve pupils in solving word problems, especially those that have more than one stage.
- Write a 'sum' on the board and ask for examples of word problems that match it.
- Check that pupils can work from their knowledge of a known number fact and place value to mentally multiply and divide.

Vocabulary
coins, total, change, pence, pound, price, cost, cheap, dear, expensive, altogether, amount, buy, spend, how much?, sell, sold, buy, bought
count on, count back, add together, take away, how much more?, method, calculate, mentally calculate, how did you work it out?
equation, equals, plus, minus, multiplication, division, addition, subtraction

Fractions

MENTAL MATHS

- Play 'show me' activities with number cards for number facts within 20. Include addition, subtraction, doubling and halving as well as solving word problems mentally.
- Ask pupils to name pairs of multiples of 100 that total 1000, such as 600 and 400.
- Ask pupils to name pairs of multiples of 5 that total 100, such as 65 and 35.
- Check that pupils can mentally multiply 2-digit multiples of 10 (to 50) by 2, 3, 4, 5 and 10, for example 30 × 2.

TEACH AND DISCUSS

Comparing and ordering fractions

Pupil's Book: page 84

- Talk about estimating the fraction shaded in each drawing at the top of the page, explaining that there are no division marks or grid lines to help.
- *Cover up fractions that you think are about one half.*
- *Cover up fractions that you think are about one third.*
- *Cover up fractions that you think are about one quarter.*
- *If one third is coloured, what fraction is not coloured?*
- *If one quarter is coloured, what fraction is not coloured?*
- Talk about the difference between situations such as halving and in two, also thirds and three parts.
- Pupils should record the fraction coloured in each shape at the bottom of the page.

Pupil's Book: page 85

- Talk about the number line at the top of the page, and half-way positions.
- Check that pupils realise that a quarter is half-way between two halves.
- Discuss equivalent fractions, such as which fractions make a whole and simple equivalents of a half.

Challenge

Decide whether the shapes to be used should be only regular or symmetrical shapes. If very irregular shapes are used then the challenge is demanding.

SUPPORTING ACTIVITIES

- Activities such as fractions dominoes could be played.
- See further activities in *Numeracy Activity Book Year 3* pages 82–87.
- Pupils play in pairs. Each takes a handful of small objects and estimates how many there are in each set. They then divide them, without counting, into what they consider to be halves. The estimations are then checked.

Vocabulary
part, equal parts, fraction, one whole, one half, two halves, one third, two-thirds, one tenth
half-way, between, nearer to
estimate, guess, about, approximately, roughly, close to, too many, not enough, too few

Time and subtracting

MENTAL MATHS

- Talk about time, which should involve telling the time, time facts such as days in a year, order of days and months and general time vocabulary.
- Ask questions that require fairly quick recall of 2, 3, 4, 5 and 10 times tables. Include complementary division facts.
- Talk about shapes and their properties. Play 'pass the parcel' with a shape. As the shape is passed along, each pupil states a different fact about the shape.
- Check that pupils can mentally multiply a 2-digit number by 2, 3, 4 or 5 where no crossing a 10 is involved, for example 23 × 2.

TEACH AND DISCUSS

Using a calendar and subtraction strategies

MAY

Mon	Tue	Wed	Thu	Fri	Sat	Sun
		1	2	3	4	5
6	7	8	9	10	11	12
13	14	15	16	17	18	19
20	21	22	23	24	25	26
27	28	29	30	31		

Pupil's Book: page 86

- Talk about calendars and what they show.
- Focus on the calendar shown on the pupil page. Explain how the arrangement is in weeks. Check that pupils know abbreviations for days of the week.
- Ask questions that involve 'one week later' and 'the week before'.
- Talk about weekends and weekdays.
- Talk about years, leap years and centuries.
- Decide whether the questions on the page are to be answered verbally or to be recorded.

Pupil's Book: page 87

- For each block of sums discuss the strategies that should be used. Include jumping along an unmarked number track. Decide whether to include more formal strategies for horizontal subtractions.
- Encourage discussion among pupils as to the strategies that can be used for the subtractions.

Challenge

Pupils should find several examples that satisfy the open problem.

SUPPORTING ACTIVITIES

- See further activities in *Numeracy Activity Book Year 3* pages 52–61.
- Write pairs of numbers on the board. Ask pupils for jumps required to show the difference between the numbers.

Vocabulary
calendar, days, weeks, months, date, century, yesterday, today, tomorrow, weekend, weekday
subtract, take away, minus, subtraction, operation, sign
method, record, draw, find a different way, how?, explain, describe, answer, check

Diagrams

MENTAL MATHS

- Talk about large numbers and how we can write them in different ways, for example 356 = 360 – 4 = 350 + 6 = 400 – 44 = …
- Ask questions that require fairly quick recall of 2, 3, 4, 5 and 10 times tables. Include complementary division facts.
- Talk about shapes and their properties. Play 'pass the parcel' with a shape. As the shape is passed along, each pupil states a different fact about the shape.
- Check that pupils can mentally multiply a 2-digit number by 2, 3, 4 or 5, where no crossing a 10 is involved, for example 23 × 2.

TEACH AND DISCUSS

Reading Venn and Carroll diagrams

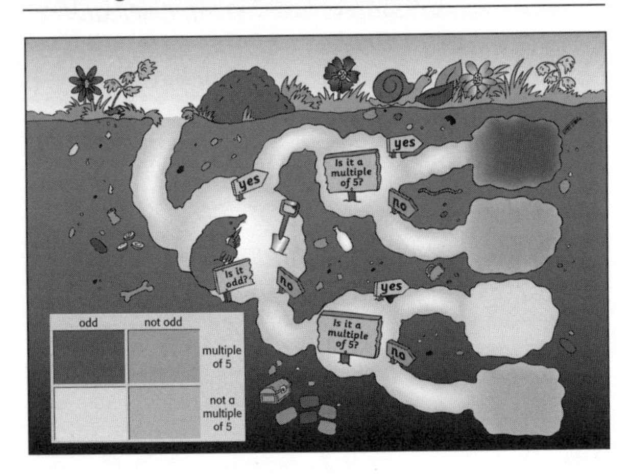

Pupil's Book: page 88

- Pupils need a set of numbers numbered 0–20 to place on the Carroll diagram. Each number should have a home on the diagram. Discuss which numbers are in each coloured block.
- Repeat, sorting these numbers using the tree diagram.
- Explain how both diagrams are sorting for the same information.
- Extend the activity to asking pupils to sort the numbers written on the page.

Pupil's Book: page 89

- Talk about Venn diagrams, explaining that the area outside the loop is just as important as the area inside the loop.

Challenge

Discuss the different ways in which the dominoes could be sorted. This might include criteria such as: doubles/not doubles; even totals/not even totals; totals more than 7/does not total more than 7.

SUPPORTING ACTIVITIES

- Any activity that involves the pupils in gathering, ordering and sorting out data.
- Use charts, diagrams, tables, adverts etc. from magazines and catalogues for pupils to discuss.
- Involve pupils in mapping, drawing rings round, ticking, etc. as part of matching information activities.

Vocabulary
Carroll diagram, Venn diagram, chart, table, graph
count, sort, vote, list, group, set, reasons, is/is not, has/has not
collect, find out, discover, choose, describe, explain, record, order, rearrange, place

Review

MENTAL MATHS

- Talk about a number chosen by the class. Pupils give as many different facts about a chosen number as possible. This could be played as 'pass the parcel'. Pupils sit in a circle and pass the number round, giving a different fact about it as it passes from pupil to pupil.
- Pupils talk about a named shape. 'Pass the parcel' with a shape should be played. A 2-D or 3-D shape is passed round the circle with a different fact being given by each pupil.
- Check quick recall of facts within 20, and multiplication tables for 2, 3, 4, 5 and 10.
- Check that pupils can add and subtract 2-digit numbers in their heads. Decide whether to include problems that involve crossing a 10.

Pupil's Book: pages 90 and 91

The pupil pages give the opportunity to assess and review:

- rounding to 100
- addition and subtraction using formal methods
- relationship between measuring units
- simple time calculations
- recognising and estimating simple fractions
- knowing table facts for 2, 3, 4, 5 and 10 times tables
- recognising right angles and quadrilaterals
- calculating change
- dividing with remainders.

Other areas for discussion should include:

Use counting skills when bridging a 10, 100 or 1000

Check that pupils can bridge when:

- adding and subtracting numbers with a range of numbers
- finding close differences.

Key vocabulary
Number *hundreds, relationship*
Measuring *litre, millilitre*
Calculation *hundreds boundary, product, method, equation*
Money *note, amount, value, expensive*
Shape *right angled, quadrilateral, map, plan, grid, row, column, angle, horizontal, vertical, diagonal*
Data handling *Venn diagram; Carroll diagram, chart, axis, axes*

TERM 1

Unit 1

1 one hundred and thirty-five
two hundred and fifty
four hundred and ninety-nine
five hundred and thirty-one

2 403 520 949 994

3 429 501 699 314

4 40 ants 100 ants 70 ants

A 1 6 2 10 3 500
4 600, 0 5 800, 5 6 300, 0
7 70, 5 8 800, 20

B 1 200 2 450 3 700 4 950
5 10 6 40 7 60 8 80

C 1 500 ml 2 700 ml 3 550 ml 4 450 ml

Challenge 6: 035 053 305 350 503 530

Unit 2

1 Both numbers must end in 5.
2 Both numbers must end in 0.
3 50 + 50
4 Other numbers must add up to 50.
5 Other numbers must add up to 95.
6 Other numbers must add up to 75.

A 1 41 2 60 3 75 4 56
5 70 6 55 7 90 8 100
9 90 10 140 11 160 12 150

B 1 In 16 and 35
Out 18 and 29
2 In 26 and 34
Out 13 and 17
3 In 3 and 13
Out 16 and 24

C 1 56 2 50 3 38 4 65
5 77 6 55 7 49 8 34

Unit 3

1 Smith 2 £1.98 3 £1.10
4 60p 5 5p

A 1 £1.55 2 £2.06 3 £1.12 4 £3.20
5 £2.02 6 £4.50 7 £2.01 8 £2.70
9 £1.22

B 1 £1.50 2 £3.75 3 40p
4 £2.80 5 £4.50

C 1 £2 2 £7.90 3 £5.20

D 1 £3.20, £1.80 2 £7.50, £2.50
3 £5.50, £4.50 4 £5.60, £4.40

Unit 4

1 4.5 cm
2 C 8.25 F 11.35
3 25 kmph
4 18 degrees
5 E 85 g G 875 g

A 1 4.10 2 9.25 3 5.40 4 2.55

B 1 5.15 2 7.35 3 10.50 4 6.05

C 1 km 2 m 3 l 4 cm 5 kg 6 g

D 20 cm

Unit 5

1 Trundle wheel 2 Height measurer
3 Tape measure 4 Depth measurer
5 Bow calliper 6 Metre stick
7 Ruler 8 Metal tape measure

A 1 6 cm 2 7 cm 3 4 cm 4 3.5 cm
5 5 cm 6 5.5 cm 7 2.5 cm 8 6 cm

B 1 1 m 55 cm 2 26 cm 3 $3\frac{1}{2}$ metres
4 20 cm 5 $1\frac{1}{2}$ metres

C 1 3 m + 20 cm, 1 m + 50 cm,
4 m + 50 cm, 2 m + 60 cm
2 50, 25, 75, 00
3 125, 475, 350, 450

Unit 6

1 Skull 2 Hut 3 Bridge
4 3 squares N, then 2 squares E
5 4 squares E, then 1 square S

B 1 hemisphere 2 pyramid 3 cylinder
4 cone 5 prism 6 cuboid

Unit 7

A **1** 400 **2** 5 **3** 70 **4** 900

B **1** 300 **2** 500 **3** 900

C **1** 21 **2** 19 **3** 9 **4** 17 **5** 21 **6** 10

D **1** £1.10 **2** £1.25 **3** £1.70

E **1** £4.40 **2** £3.50 **3** £1.50 **4** £2.30

F **1** 9.25 **2** 2.40 **3** ten o'clock **4** quarter past twelve

G **1** 5 cm **2** 5 cm **3** 7 cm **4** 6 cm

H **1** 320 **2** 105 **3** 225 **4** 575

I **1** hemisphere **2** pyramid **3** cuboid **4** cylinder **5** prism

Unit 8

1 51, 53, 55, 57, 59
2 72, 74, 76, 78, 80, 82, 84, 86, 88
3 40, 45, 50, 55, 60, 65, 70
4 15, 21, 27
5 96

A **1** 44 **2** 39 **3** 80 **4** 55

B **1** 43, 53, 63 **2** 56, 46, 36 **3** 145, 155, 165 **4** 356, 346, 336

C **1** 48, 50, 52 **2** 73, 75, 77 **3** 99, 101, 103 **4** 93, 95, 97 **5** 64, 66, 68 **6** 50, 52, 54

D Odd numbers: 9, 11, 15
Multiples of 3: 6, 9, 12, 15
Both: 9, 15
Neither: 8

Challenge True.

Unit 9

2 16 **3** 6 **4** 90
5 2×18, 3×12, 4×9, 6×6

A **1** 10, 16, 15, 30, 45
2 4, 9, 3, 7, 9
3 5, 10, 6, 9, 3

B **1** 8, 4, 3, 7, 10
2 5, 5, 2, 5, 10
3 10, 30, 70, 15, 32

C **1** 14 **2** 12 **3** 60 **4** 18 **5** 15 **6** 9 **7** 7 **8** 5 **9** 4 **10** 6

D **1** 35p **2** £20 **3** 6 **4** 10

Unit 10

1 £9 **2** £12 **3** £20 **4** 4 **5** 3

A **1** 30 **2** 24 **3** 40 **4** 60

B **1** 90 **2** 110 **3** 190 **4** 240 **5** 290 **6** 300 **7** 360 **8** 750 **9** 910 **10** 590 **11** 410 **12** 500 **13** 730 **14** 460 **15** 870 **16** 990

C **1** 16, 24, 28, 32, 40 **2** 5, 10, 15, 4, 6

D **1** 24 **2** 44 **3** 30 **4** 60 **5** 160 **6** 120 **7** 100 **8** 180

Challenge
$4 \times 6 = 24$ $3 \times 9 = 27$
$6 \times 4 = 24$ $9 \times 3 = 27$
$24 \div 6 = 4$ $27 \div 9 = 3$
$24 \div 4 = 6$ $27 \div 3 = 9$

Unit 11

1 B **2** E **3** D **4** F **5** C

A **1** $\frac{1}{5}$ **2** $\frac{1}{4}$ **3** $\frac{1}{3}$ **4** $\frac{1}{3}$

B **1** 4, 6, 9, 12, 15 **2** 2, 5, 7, 9, 10 **3** 2, 4, 3, 5, 9 **4** 2, 4, 5, 8, 10

C **1** $3\frac{1}{2}$ **2** $4\frac{1}{2}$ **3** $6\frac{1}{2}$ **4** $9\frac{1}{2}$ **5** £1.50 **6** £2.50 **7** £4.50 **8** £5.50

Unit 12

1 30 minutes **2** 10.10
3 11.45 **4** 30 minutes
5 2.45 **6** 35 minutes
7 $1\frac{1}{2}$ hours **8** 13 hours

A **1** 20, 34, 65, 70
2 12, 24, 32, 66
3 0, 4, 30, 73

B **1** 24, 37 **2** 82, 57 **3** 49, 73

C **1** 5 **2** 9 **3** 7 **4** 7 **5** 5

D **1** 9 **2** 44 **3** 20 **4** 32 **5** 49

Unit 13

1 11 **2** Joe and Sarah **3** Mai and Ian
4 6 **5** Ian

A 1 Orange **2** Purple **3** $3\frac{1}{2}$ **4** $5\frac{1}{2}$ **5** 4

Unit 14

C 18, 45, 14

D 5, 2, 5

E 2, 10, 0

F 4, 6, 9

G 20, 24, 30, 50, 80, 70

H 20, 15, $2\frac{1}{2}$, $4\frac{1}{2}$, $8\frac{1}{2}$, 12

I 2 and 3

J 1 $\frac{3}{10}$ **2** $\frac{3}{4}$ **3** $\frac{2}{3}$ **4** $\frac{3}{5}$

K 1 $\frac{1}{2}$ **2** $\frac{1}{6}$ **3** $\frac{1}{4}$ **4** $\frac{1}{3}$

L 1 26, 48 **2** 91, 72 **3** 18, 52

M 9.30

N 35

O 150, 300, 750, 460, 710

TERM 2

Unit 1

A 1 20 **2** 40 **3** 40 **4** 60
5 60, 70 **6** 80 **7** 80, 90 **8** 100

B 1 20 **2** 45 **3** 65 **4** 82 **5** 99

C 1 70 g **2** 160 g **3** 45 g **4** 185 g

Challenge 300, 210, 201, 120, 102, 30, 21, 12, 3

Unit 2

1 75, 53, 45, 84, 62
2 16, 13, 6, 9, 11
3 46, 39, 57, 67, 82

A 1 15 **2** 21 **3** 21 **4** 16 **5** 21
6 17 **7** 19 **8** 26 **9** 23 **10** 21
11 24 **12** 25

B 1 18 **2** 19 **3** 18 **4** 27 **5** 29
6 20 **7** 21 **8** 24 **9** 30 **10** 30

C 1 76 **2** 74 **3** 91 **4** 69 **5** 95
6 79 **7** 77 **8** 77 **9** 89 **10** 89
11 60 **12** 60 **13** 80 **14** 80 **15** 90

D 1 84 **2** 57 **3** 72 **4** 85 **5** 95
6 96 **7** 62 **8** 82 **9** 92 **10** 88
11 91 **12** 93 **13** 95 **14** 92 **15** 83

Challenge 1 66 **2** 55 **3** 47 **4** 43 **5** 27
6 113 **7** 152 **8** 123 **9** 183 **10** 121

Unit 3

A 1 –, + **2** –, + **3** +, – **4** +, + **5** –, –
6 +, – **7** +, – **8** –, + **9** +, +

B 1 5 **2** 85 **3** 99 **4** 62 **5** 73
6 23 **7** 14 **8** 45 **9** 48 **10** 62
11 84 **12** 96 **13** 81 **14** 74 **15** 42

C 1 397 **2** 219 **3** 508 **4** 647 **5** 879
6 385 **7** 492 **8** 720 **9** 892 **10** 642
11 650 **12** 580 **13** 320 **14** 650 **15** 540

D 1 436 **2** 754 **3** 296 **4** 517 **5** 692
6 298 **7** 394 **8** 895 **9** 797 **10** 196
11 700 **12** 800 **13** 1000 **14** 900 **15** 900

Unit 4

1 60p **2** £1.60 **3** £2.10 **4** £2.80 **5** £1.85
6 £3.50 **7** £2.25 **8** £1.80 **9** £3.10 **10** £2.10

A 1 33 **2** 24 **3** 96 **4** 3

B 1 £1.50, 50p **2** 50p **3** £1.50
4 4 **5** Mandy 50p, Li 40p **6** £1.05

C 120p, 475p, 306p, 710p, 936p, 886p
£3.04, £8.14, £7.00, £4.75, £6.39, £9.99

Unit 5

B 1 rhombus **2** hexagon **3** square
4 oval **5** triangle

Unit 6

A 2.25 **B** 3.45 **C** 4.55 **D** 7.30

E 1.05 **F** 3.10 **G** 10.15 **H** 11.35

1 8.30 **2** 4.10 **3** H **4** E **5** 35 minutes

A 1 2 **2** 5 **3** 10 **4** 20

B 1 2 kg **2** $4\frac{1}{2}$ kg **3** $\frac{1}{2}$ kg **4** nearly 3 kg

C **1** 1000 g, 500 g, 2000 g
2 1200 g, 2500 g, 3250 g
3 1 kg, 1 kg 200 g, 1 kg 300 g

D **1** Louise **2** Sunita **3** 3 kg **4** 2 kg

Unit 7

A 80, 40, 50 or 60, 80, 100

B **1** 20 **2** 60 **3** 75 **4** 92

C **1** 22 **2** 23

D **1** 55 **2** 59 **3** 70

E **1** 61 **2** 92 **3** 93

F **1** 74 **2** 12 **3** 81

G **1** £7.50 **2** £2.50

H **1** rectangle **2** triangle **3** oval
4 semicircle **5** pentagon

I **1** cuboid **2** hemisphere **3** prism
4 pyramid **5** cylinder

J **1** 1.25 **2** 3.55 **3** 2.50 **4** 10.10

K **1** 5 cm **2** 9 cm **3** 9 cm

Unit 8

1 999 **2** 110
3 110, 210, 250, 305, 375, 400, 450, 500, 550, 645, 700
4 110, 210, 250, 400, 450, 500, 550, 700
5 400, 500, 700
6 852
7 110, 176, 199, 210, 250, 289
8 803, 852, 999
9 450, 457
10 199, 999

A **1** 75, 85, 95, 105
2 67, 77, 87, 97
3 104, 114, 124, 134
4 98, 108, 118, 128
5 101, 111, 121, 131
6 155, 165, 175, 185
7 236, 246, 256, 266
8 408, 418, 428, 438
9 793, 803, 813, 823
10 900, 910, 920, 930

B **1** 50, 129, 212, 203, 300
2 87, 179, 310, 301, 397
3 82, 150, 214, 462, 600

Unit 9

1 14 and 86, 25 and 75, 40 and 60, 45 and 55
4 113 **5** 54 **6** 109

B **1** 84 **2** 85 **3** 75 **4** 76 **5** 90
6 91 **7** 83 **8** 80 **9** 89 **10** 58

C **1** 122 **2** 110 **3** 120 **4** 132 **5** 161
6 160 **7** 139 **8** 161 **9** 128 **10** 121

D **1** 45 **2** 51 **3** 55 **4** 69 **5** 74
6 69 **7** 70 **8** 106

E **1** £49 **2** £1.48 **3** £1.50
4 £13.50 **5** £3.75 **6** 5

Unit 10

A **1** 5 **2** 3 **3** 4 **4** 5 **5** 6 **6** 8
7 9 **8** 7 **9** 10 **10** 9 **11** 8 **12** 8

B **1** 8 **2** 20 **3** 12 **4** 16 **5** 24
6 32 **7** 45 **8** 24 **9** 21 **10** 20

C **1** 2 **2** 3 **3** 4 **4** 5 **5** 5
6 3 **7** 4 **8** 3 **9** 2 **10** 4

D **1** £6 **2** £6 **3** £4 **4** £9
5 12 **6** 11 **7** 12 **8** 13
9 Yes **10** No **11** Yes **12** No

E 6, 10, 14, 18 6, 18, 27, 30 5, 20, 25, 35

Unit 11

A **1** $\frac{1}{2}$ **2** $\frac{1}{4}$ **3** $\frac{1}{10}$ **4** $\frac{1}{3}$ **5** $\frac{3}{4}$

B **1** 2 **2** 4 **3** 10 **4** 2 **5** 5

C **1** 50 **2** 25 **3** 4 **4** 15

Unit 12

1 Red **2** Green **3** 3
4 3 **5** 4 **6** 12

A **1** 6 **2** blue tit **3** robin
4 9 **5** 3 **6** 30

B **1** cola **2** 10 **3** 5
4 3 **5** 6 **6** 49

Unit 13

A **1** 40 **2** 70 **3** 60 or 70 **4** 90 **5** 90

B **1** 45 **2** 120 **3** 86 **4** 65

C **1** £4.50 **2** £2.60 **3** £7 **4** £2

D 1, 2, 5

E **1** 45 **2** 68 **3** 22 **4** 79

F **1** 5 cm **2** $2\frac{1}{2}$ cm **3** 6 cm

G **1** 70 **2** 12 **3** 25 **4** 18
5 3 **6** 7 **7** 10 **8** 9

H **1** 6 **2** 5 **3** 8 **4** 2
5 20 **6** 16 **7** 2 **8** 10

I **1** $\frac{1}{2}$ **2** $\frac{3}{4}$ **3** $\frac{2}{3}$ **4** $\frac{1}{10}$

J **1** 5.35 **2** 950 ml **3** $5\frac{1}{2}$ kg

TERM 3

Unit 1

2 253, 367, 670, 402, 897

3 500, 70, 2, 60, 700 and 9

A **1** 300 **2** 400 **3** 900 **4** 600 or 700
5 200 **6** 600 **7** 800 **8** 900 or 1000

B **1** 200 **2** 300 **3** 400 **4** 500
5 600 **6** 800 **7** 300 **8** 800

C **1** £5 **2** £4 **3** £6 **4** £7 or £8
5 £2 **6** £3 **7** £7 **8** £5

D **1** 100 **2** 250 **3** 550 **4** 720 **5** 980

Unit 2

1 65 **2** 45 **3** 76 **4** 75 **5** 77
6 87 **7** 89 **8** 143 **9** 87 **10** 115
11 48 **12** 108 **13** 118 **14** 148 **15** 188

A **1** 21 **2** 25 **3** 28 **4** 20
5 27 **6** 28 **7** 28 **8** 28

B **1** 800 **2** 100 **3** 500 **4** 600 **5** 900
6 700 **7** 400 **8** 200 **9** 300 **10** 600

C **1** 5, 15, 25, 35, 45
2 5, 15, 25, 35, 45
3 4, 40, 400, 80, 8

D **1** 1100, 1400, 1400, 1100
2 596, 393, 291, 795
3 327, 436, 745, 897

Unit 3

1 3 **2** 8 **3** 5 **4** 10 **5** 4
6 30p **7** 33p **8** 30p **9** £9 **10** £4.60

A **1** £5.90 **2** £1.50 **3** £1.03

C **1** £3.80 **2** £7.50 **3** 4, 4p
4 £2.40 **5** 12p **6** £1.40

D **1** 55p **2** 42p **3** 37p **4** 81p **5** 74p **6** 23p

Unit 4

1 108, 110, 114
2 377, 380, 384
3 736, 766, 770, 772
4 60, 3, 2
5 60, 2, 5
6 200, 40, 3

A **1** 143 **2** 113 **3** 95 **4** 112 **5** 123
6 102 **7** 104 **8** 133 **9** 136 **10** 101

B **1** 294 **2** 243 **3** 295 **4** 501 **5** 595
6 335 **7** 223 **8** 696 **9** 553 **10** 862

C **1** 577 **2** 603 **3** 419 **4** 790 **5** 610
6 950 **7** 658 **8** 684

D **1** 91 **2** 95 **3** 123 **4** 122 **5** 135
6 130 **7** 143 **8** 121 **9** 120 **10** 81

E **1** 205 **2** 615 **3** 675 **4** 384 **5** 782
6 334 **7** 646 **8** 533 **9** 463 **10** 811

Unit 5

A **1** 700 ml **2** 100 ml **3** 850 ml **4** 750 ml

B **1** 650 ml **2** 150 ml **3** 900 ml
4 250 ml **5** 1

C **1** 3 **2** 15 days

Unit 6

1 Caravan site, Canoes, Farm

2 D1, G1, C4

Unit 7

A **1** 400 or 500 **2** 300 **3** 300 **4** 900 **5** 700

B 237, 273, 327, 372, 723, 732

C **1** 28 **2** 29 **3** 30

D About 120, 350, 595, 855

E **1** 800 **2** 1000 **3** 1500

F **1** 93 **2** 92 **3** 130 **4** 151

G **1** 185 **2** 443 **3** 694 **4** 814

H **1** 4.25 **2** 6.50 **3** 10.55

I **1** cuboid **2** prism **3** hemisphere
4 pyramid **5** triangle **6** quadrilateral
7 pentagon **8** hexagon

Unit 8

1 525 **2** 990 **3** 450 and 550, 750 and 250
4 525, 550, 640 **5** 150, 175, 208, 236, 250
6 150, 208, 236, 250, 300, 310, 380, 400, 410, 446, 450, 550, 640, 720, 750, 950, 990
7 All *except* 208, 236, 446
8 All numbers ending in 0.
9 150, 250, 300, 400, 450, 550, 750, 950
10 300, 400

A **1** 76, 78, 80 **2** 75, 70, 65 **3** 165, 170, 175
4 46, 49, 52 **5** 78, 75, 72

B **1** Multiples of 5: 60, 75, 135, 205, 765
Not multiples of 5: 54, 352, 556

2 Multiples of 2: 64, 86, 198, 310, 652
Not multiples of 2: 45, 253, 999

C **1** True **2** True **3** Not true **4** True

Challenge $2 + 3 + 4 = 9$
$3 + 4 + 5 + 6 = 18$
$6 + 7 + 8 = 21$
$5 + 6 + 7 + 8 = 26$

Unit 9

A **1** 5 r.1 **2** 7 r.1 **3** 3 r.2 **4** 4 r.1 **5** 4 r.3
6 3 r.7 **7** 5 r.3 **8** 7 r.6 **9** 6 r.1 **10** 8 r.2
11 9 r.1 **12** 8 r.4 **13** 8 r.2 **14** 6 r.1 **15** 9 r.9

B **1** 4 r.4 **2** 7 r.5 **3** 3 r.6 **4** 8 r.£1
5 6 r.1 **6** 7 r.0 **7** 6 r.2 **8** 7 r.2
9 6 r.1 **10** 4 r.30p

C **1** 7 **2** 8 **3** 3 **4** 5

D **1** 10 **2** 5

Challenge $56 = 10 \times 5 + 6$ $87 = 10 \times 8 + 7$
$19 = 5 \times 3 + 4$ $48 = 9 \times 5 + 3$
$25 = 6 \times 4 + 1$ $93 = 10 \times 9 + 3$

Unit 10

1 £1, £1, 5p **2** £2, £1, 10p
3 50p, 50p, 2p **4** 20p, 20p, 20p
5 £1, 50p, 20p **6** £2, £2, 50p, 50p
7 £2, 50p, 50p, 50p **8** 50p, 20p, 20p, 10p
9 50p, 50p, 5p, 1p **10** £2, 50p, 20p, 10p

A **1** 700, 300, 500, 800, 600
2 7, 9, 2, 4, 3
3 10, 50, 60, 80, 70
4 10, 100, 100, 10, 10

B

In	15	20	35	45	50
Out	30	40	70	90	100

In	30	40	50	80	90
Out	15	20	25	40	45

C **1** 120 **2** 5 **3** 70 **4** 10
5 96 **6** 2 **7** 11 **8** 2

D 100, 69, 3

Challenge $320 \div 10 = 32$ $400 - 40 = 360$
$50 \times 30 = 1500$ $200 + 600 = 800$
$240 \div 20 = 12$ $700 \div 2 = 350$

Unit 11

1 $\frac{1}{2}$ **2** $\frac{1}{10}$ **3** $\frac{2}{8}$ or $\frac{1}{4}$ **4** $\frac{1}{2}$ **5** $\frac{1}{3}$ **6** $\frac{1}{3}$

A **1** $1\frac{1}{2}$ **2** $3\frac{1}{2}$ **3** $\frac{3}{4}$ **4** $2\frac{1}{4}$ **5** 2 **6** 2

B **1** 30 **2** 35 **3** 15 **4** 40 **5** 12 **6** 34

C **1** $\frac{2}{2}$ **2** $\frac{3}{3}$ **3** $\frac{4}{4}$ **4** $\frac{10}{10}$
5 $\frac{2}{4}$ **6** $\frac{5}{10}$ **7** $\frac{1}{2}$ **8** $\frac{3}{4}$

Unit 12

1 Wednesday **2** 21st **3** 29th May
4 4th/5th **5** Saturday **6** Tuesday

A **1** 80, 40, 86, 61
2 40, 110, 50, 110
3 130, 150, 138, 124

B 1 15 2 18 3 55 4 37 5 49
6 47 7 36 8 36 9 29 10 39

C 1 28 2 44 3 15 4 49 5 26
6 46 7 45 8 19 9 66 10 28

D 1 106 2 229 3 387 4 515 5 615
6 184 7 355 8 734 9 544 10 664

Unit 13

1 red 2 blue 3 yellow 4 green
5 blue 6 blue 7 green 8 red
9 yellow 10 green

A 1 yellow 2 blue 3 yellow 4 blue
5 blue 6 yellow 7 blue 8 yellow
9 blue 10 yellow

B 1 red 2 green 3 green 4 red
5 green 6 red 7 red 8 green

Unit 14

A 1 500 2 300 or 400 3 500
4 400 5 800

B 1 84 2 35 3 317 4 248

C 1 1000 ml 2 500 g 3 1000 m

D 1 4.25 2 4.35 3 11.05 4 5.20

E 1 $\frac{1}{4}$ 2 $\frac{1}{2}$ 3 $\frac{1}{3}$ 4 $\frac{1}{10}$

F 1 9 2 7 3 2 4 4

G 1 5 2 3 3 80 4 16

H 1 and 5

All *except* 1

I 1 £5.30 2 £3.75 3 £2.25 4 £7.01

Pupil's Book: pages 92 to 95

At the back of the Pupil's Books are four pages of glossary items:

- Number bonds – addition bonds and multiplication bonds
- Shapes – two- and three-dimensional shapes
- Angles and direction – turns, directions and angles
- Time and measures – relationships between measuring units.

Pupils should be trained to look at these pages when they need to find something out. They can also be used as discussion pages during the plenary sessions.